refabricating
ARCHITECTURE

refabricating
ARCHITECTURE

How Manufacturing Methodologies Are
Poised to Transform Building Construction

Stephen Kieran James Timberlake

McGraw-Hill

New York Chicago San Francisco Lisbon
London Madrid Mexico City Milan New Delhi
San Juan Seoul Singapore Sydney Toronto

Cataloging-in-Publication Data is on file with the Library of Congress.

3 4 5 6 7 8 9 0   DOC/DOC   0 9 8 7 6 5 4

ISBN 0-07-143321-X

The sponsoring editor for this book was Cary Sullivan, the editing supervisor was Caroline Levine, and the production supervisor was Sherri Souffrance.

Printed and bound by RR Donnelley.

 This book is printed on recycled, acid-free paper containing a minimum of 50 percent recycled de-inked fiber.

McGraw-Hill books are available at special quantity discounts to use as premiums and sales promotions, or for use in corporate training programs. For more information, please write to the Director of Special Sales, McGraw-Hill Professional, Two Penn Plaza, New York, NY 10121-2298. Or contact your local bookstore.

For Barbara, Christopher, Caitlin and
Marguerite, Harrison and Veronica

CONTENTS

ACKNOWLEDGMENTS

A book of this nature is not the work of the authors alone. Research on the concepts behind *refabricating Architecture* began within our University of Pennsylvania Master of Architecture Research Laboratory. The many students that we have had during the past four years have contributed to the opportunities presented by the challenges this book addresses. We extend our thanks for their insight and hard work. Dean Gary Hack and Richard Wesley, the former Chair of the Department of Architecture within the School of Design, have substantially supported the work in our laboratory. It has enabled doors to be opened anew and innovative walls to be constructed involving technologies seen and unseen.

The College of Fellows of the American Institute of Architects awarded us the inaugural Benjamin Latrobe Research Fellowship in 2001 for a proposal which has become this book. We are grateful to the College and their first jury of Harold Roth, Cesar Pelli, Harry Cobb, Harrison Fraker, and Charles Redmon for their faith in the promise of the proposal and our work. From that initial grant we were able to incorporate a research agenda into our office. At this writing this agenda has shown results with four architects dedicated to research topics ranging from off-site fabrications to innovative wall assemblies and interior components employing new ways of assembly and materiality.

Our research has taken us to near and far places. In Ridley, Pennsylvania and Everett, Washington we were given extensive time and tours of Boeing assembly plants. Bob Young and Tom Strevey were our hosts and guides. They have been immensely helpful to us with additional materials, images, and information. Similarly, in Detroit, Paul Kleppert and Ray Shashaani at DaimlerChrysler initiated us into the moments of process engineering. They sent us to Toledo, Ohio; we met with Ted Roberts and toured the DCX Jeep Liberty and Wrangler plants. These are plants where new and old world manufacturing exist side-by-side. Distant were memories of the 1960s tours of the River Rouge plant which loomed large in the comparative thoughts we took away from our tour. Vince Brooks, Design Chief at Delphi Systems in Troy, Michigan, has provided ongoing insight into how the automotive industry has turned its world upside down in the past decade. In Philadelphia, we have twice visited the Kvaerner Philadelphia shipyard, a new technology yard where the first container ship built on the East Coast of the United States in nearly four decades is nearing completion. Jennifer Whitener led us through tours of their innovative operation, answered questions, and supplied images. We could not have tested our theory without having access to these corporations.

There are individuals who have provoked us with their thoughts and the opportunities that they saw in our thesis. They have each caused us to think differently about our different thinking. These include James Becker of Skanska USA, Dave Richards of Arup, Norbert Young of McGraw-Hill, Sara Hart and Charles Linn of Architectural Record, and Marc Zobec of Permasteelisa. Collective intelligence is good.

We have a wonderful group of collaborators near us in Philadelphia. Our office. No more creative and energetic place exists. Without the dedication of our staff on a daily basis these ideas would remain dormant: unwritten, unsaid, unenacted. Jonathan Fallet began the work. No one has done more than Richard Seltenrich in working at and on the ideas of the book, crafting imagery, extending the potential and provoking further thought. Sarah Williams has, off-site refabricated our words into proper text. Karl Wallick, an invaluable collaborator and contributor, has worked with us closely since participating in the initial research studio four years ago. His contributions may be seen woven into the workings of all the research studios, in the crafting of SmartWrap at the Cooper Hewitt Museum, and in the words and images of this book. He has been pivotal in the execution and extension of our research and practice agenda into refabricating Architecture.

Lastly, our families have given us space to grow, learn, and expand our passion for architecture. We are grateful to them for their presence in our lives and for waiting for us.

"Architecture or revolution. Revolution can be avoided."
Le Corbusier

ARGUMENT

The architect awakes from an 80-year dream to find that sleep has never really come. All appears different yet is in fact the same. Beneath the veneer of the new is an all too familiar world. Appearance has triumphed over substance. Architecture still takes years—many years—to design and build. Architecture still requires resources out of all proportion to outcome, and this requirement places it beyond the means of most of humanity. Quality continues its long decline. Few truly new materials, features, and processes have become commonplace.

Our newly awakened architect compares this state of affairs to advances in the design and fabrication of automobiles, airplanes, and ships. In these constructions, new materials and processes abound. Fabrication times have decreased along with production cost and waste, while quality has increased exponentially. New scope and new features, inconceivable advances that meet the eye, require explanation because their novelty has no parallel to earlier experience.

In these fields, the process engineer has triumphed, while in building, the architect continues to decline. The architect remains content, apparently, to focus on the appearance of things, while the process engineer goes beyond appearance into the deepest substance of making to invert the historic, craft-based relations between cost and time, on the one hand, and scope and quality, on the other. For the process engineer, the act of design has extended beyond the assembly line to the complete life-cycle of products. While the world of architecture has grown ever more wasteful, disposable, splintered, and specialized, the process engineer flourishes in the fluid integration of makers by dissolving, not reinforcing, boundaries between thinkers and makers. The world wants to know: Why does architecture remain immune to transformation and progress? Why is it that the master builders of today arise from the ranks of the process engineer, not the architect?

Hundreds of years ago, all of architecture could be held in the intelligence of a single maker, the master builder. Part architect, part builder, part product and building engineer, and part materials scientist, the master builder integrated all the elements of architecture in a single mind, heart, and hand. The most significant, yet troubling, legacy of modernism has been the specialization of the various elements of building once directed and harmonized by the master builder. The multiple foci at the core of specialization have given rise to a world that is advancing while fragmenting. We applaud the advancement, but deplore a fragmentation that is no longer unavoidable and so needlessly diminishes architecture. Today, through the agency of information management tools, the architect can once again become the master builder by integrating the skills and intelligences at the core of architecture. This new master builder transforms the singular mind glorified in schools and media to a new genius of collective intelligence. Today's master architect is an amalgam of material scientist, product engineer, process engineer, user, and client who creates architecture informed by commodity and art. By recognizing commodity as an equal partner to art, architecture is made as accessible, affordable, and sustainable as the most technically sophisticated consumer products available today.

All complex human endeavors, including architecture, require a regulating structure to organize the inherent chaos that underlies its making. Our regulatory structures today are information management tools, not the idealized mathematical constructs of classical architecture. Modern humanism is communication, not geometry. Communication tools allow architects and our collaborators to conceive, discuss, explore, and understand every detail before we produce it. The process is accessible to all, including the user and client. Architects are no longer limited to the fragmentary representation of physical ideas; we can now fully pre-form them. This composite understanding of architecture before it actually becomes substance offers a deep understanding of the elements of architecture that affect our daily lives. Refabricating architecture leads toward a new humanism.

What has changed today? Everything. Mass production was the ideal of the early twentieth century. Mass customization is the recently emerged reality of the twenty-first century. We have always customized architecture to recognize differences. Customization ran at cross purpose to the twentieth-century model of mass production. Mass customization is a hybrid. It proposes new processes to build using automated production, but with the ability to differentiate each artifact from those that are fabricated before and after. The ability to differentiate, to distinguish architecture based upon site, use, and desire, is a prerequisite to success that has eluded our predecessors. With the information control tools we now have we are able to visualize and manage off-site fabrication of mass customized architecture. Architecture has over the past century finally become a machine, with as much as fifty percent of the cost embedded in systems, not structure, walls, and roof. Developments of lightweight, high-strength, and high-performance materials offer the prospect of economy, efficient transport, re-use, and less waste all of which streamline the process cycle. The result is a more sustainable architecture. Architects, constructors, and clients reap the rewards.

There are few revolutions in the making of things. Here, change is almost always a matter of gradual movement from one manner of making and appearance to another. Change in the making of architecture, in its unseen processes, is already here. It is arriving first in modest ways, increasingly in more transparent examples. There are few epiphanies in the processes of architecture, only a dawning realization that things are not the same. The laws of economics demand more continuity than discontinuity in the making of architecture for both consumer and maker, but the infrastructure and the will to evolve is already here among us. The architect awakes.

1

THE PROCESS ENGINEER AND THE AESTHETICS OF ARCHITECTURE

 **OR**

ART/commodity   **COMMODITY/art**

IS ARCHITECTURE ART OR A COMMODITY   *Currently, little architecture is intended to be both art and commodity, but rather a commodity of value serving a specific function and purpose. It is almost solely utilitarian. Art has become an expensive luxury, included only when it has an economic value.*

 **AND**

ART/COMMODITY   **COMMODITY/ART**

ARCHITECTURE THAT IS SIMULTANEOUSLY ART AND A COMMODITY   *The Parthenon of the ancient Greeks and Le Corbusier's grain towers have achieved a status of both art and commodity, breaking the typical dichotomy in architecture.*

1.1   ARCHITECTURE: ART OR COMMODITY

Choice often strengthens. The choice art *or* commodity weakens. Why not art *and* commodity? Never has the distance between the two positions been so great. Never before has the practice of architecture so hardened the lines of debate between its aspiration to become an art and its acceptance as a commodity. Clients and even architects demand that we choose: art or commodity. Few buildings elevate architecture to art and so move the soul.

Art and commodity, once the double soul of architecture, have now split and succumbed to specialization. Choose your world.

Architecture can be art. It can, in some circumstances, come to exist in an elevated realm—an art market beyond the general economy. Or, architecture can be a commodity, an artifact of use to be bought and sold in accordance with prevailing principles of economic exchange. Only rarely, here at the opening of the twenty-first century, is architecture both art and commodity. The rest merely provide shelter with a minimum of means.

Commodity was once—and can be again—the tollgate on the way to art. Commodity was once the great editor, the test of optimum fitness no matter what the resources. The Parthenon is great in part because it is lean, because it passes all the tests of a minimum expenditure of resources to effect the maximum gain. In it there is no stone that does not speak of its passage from purpose to desire to shaping in accordance with both craft and economy of means.

Commodity was once equated with the traditions of craft present in architecture that became art. Craft itself was the web of knowledge about putting things together that one negotiated on the way to economy. New ways of assembling were continually invented and refined over time to effect higher quality and greater economy. Evolutionary change in vernacular building is a record of lean thought that becomes poetic by virtue of its fitness.

COMMODITY/ART   ART/COMMODITY

A COMMODITY OF VALUE HAD TO BE HANDCRAFTED   *Before the twentieth century, the more human energy that was invested in an architectural work, the greater its value. Since excess of handcraft was an indulgence, anything extra represented great expense and effort.*

 **VS.**

AESTHETIC   FUNCTION

ENGINEERS ARE NOT GUIDED BY PRECONCEPTION ABOUT APPEARANCE   *Robert Venturi places an emphasis upon the aesthetics of iconography and semiotics, while the engineer lets form follow function. (Image: courtesy Office of the Secretary of Air Force Public Affairs.)*

1.2   THE HAND AND THE MACHINE

Making by hand was the only way we had of fabricating artifacts for most of our history. It required a great expenditure of human energy. When things were made by hand, economies in the expenditure of this energy came about naturally. The designer was often one and the same with the maker. The barn was designed by those who raised and used it; the factory was designed by the engineer or owner who built it. Building was at one with the laws of economy. When thinking and making were thus bound together, the economy of pure form that we associate with vernacular building was sure to follow.

The Hand and the Machine. Handcraft was once the tool of commodity, but today it is the machine that is the tool of commodity.

The transition from handcraft to machine-craft was a dream of modernist thought throughout the twentieth century. Many of the most significant architects of the twentieth century pursued this dream of machine production. The goal was to make some architecture, especially housing, into a commodity for consumption by the masses. Handcraft is now an indulgence left over from another century.

The twentieth century's fascination with vernacular architecture arose from an understanding of the shaping power of economic forces in the construction industry. The power of vernacular construction is a direct result of the connection between need, design, and making in these straightforward buildings. A steady stream of modernist architectural thought sought ways to translate this directness into the economies of industrial production and thereby to direct the vernacular methods of the twentieth century.

When Le Corbusier praised grain silos and factories because their pure form had been shaped by the economic rules of production, he came down in favor of engineers. They are the unselfconscious makers, he told us, the vernacular architects and producers of modern

ART/COMMODITY
handcraft

ART/COMMODITY
mass production

MECHANIZATION TAKES COMMAND   *The twentieth century saw machine production establish itself as an art form of commercial and artistic value. Nonhandcrafted processes became both a requirement and an indulgence.*

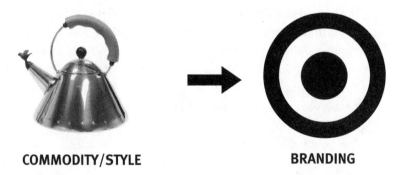

COMMODITY/STYLE

BRANDING

COMMODIFICATION LEADS TO BRANDING   *The extreme marketing and mass production of an artifact leads to a common recognizability and an expected value. The artifact transcends art and commodity to become solely a product, reducing the architect/ designer to mere stylist.*

form. For Le Corbusier, engineers, unlike architects, are not guided by preconception about appearance. Instead, they possess a single-minded focus on purpose and economy. Poetic mass, surface, and plan result from the filters of economics and process through which their projects must pass.

Le Corbusier saw great promise in the production of architecture by machines, particularly in housing where it offered a way to fulfill a social housing agenda. Economic and social agendas were merged with construction and architecture in his vision of a vernacular.

—————

Architecture produced as an industrial product would naturally become a new vernacular.

It would be art because of its very lack of pretension. The way to art in much twentieth-century theory and practice would be by means of a thorough transformation of production. Architecture as a mass-produced product would transform both access and perception; it would become a thing, a commodity, a vernacular shelter for the twentieth century. Great architecture is today equated with art. Commodity today is generally seen as anti-art, the stuff of commerce. Commodity, most believe, is the creed of the philistine. It is possible, however, to see commodity instead as the crucible of art itself and to recognize the process engineer—not the design engineer—as the high priest of this new art. It is not the engineer as a designer of artifacts that we applaud, but rather as a designer of processes that show the way forward in art.

The design of how we go about designing, and ultimately making, circumscribes what we make. It controls the art found in its quality, scope, or features and also the resources of time and money expended on its production. This reality is completely contrary to the artistic and contractual structure of much current architecture, which specifically excludes the architect from participation in the "means and methods" of making, thus turning architects into mere stylists.

Q <small>x</small> S = C <small>x</small> T

Quality   Scope   Cost   Time

THE FORMULA OF ARCHITECTURAL PRODUCTION *The current paradigm in architecture is that quality and scope are directly proportional to the cost and time to execute.*

1.3   THE LAW OF ECONOMY AND VALUE

What are the rules that circumscribe this new specialist, the process engineer? Process engineering has, in the past, been bound by a simple yet seemingly ineluctable equation:

$$Q(uality) \times S(cope) = C(ost) \times T(ime)$$

Quality and scope are generally desirable aspects of anything we make. We like things that are well made. When they are well made, we say they are crafted. We also like added features and generally wish for more rather than less. Cost and time, however, are not desirable elements. They are the limits that determine how much quality and scope we can attain. While we might want more quality and scope, we still want to spend less time and money. In classical process-engineering terms, the way to attain a certain combination of higher quality and greater scope is to spend some combination of more time and more money.

THE NEW CLIENT MANDATE *The design and execution of architecture is increasingly subject to a new rule of economy. Architects find themselves having to increase quality and scope disproportionately to the execution cost and time consumed. Clients are demanding more for less.*

1.4   A NEW CLIENT MANDATE

While architecture has passively accepted this equation as universal law, as though it were a force of nature, other industries have refused to do so. The process engineer lives to obliterate the equilibrium of this law, to relegate it to the dustbin of history.

The process engineer is the force that moves the automotive, shipbuilding, and aircraft industries beyond the gravitational fields of cost and time and into realms where quality and scope can increase out of all proportion to cost and time, where art transcends resources.

Q(uality) × S(cope) › C(ost) × T(ime)

Why is this restatement, this reprieve from the old equilibrium between art and expenditure, possible in other industries that also make complex artifacts? Cars, ships, and planes must even move through space, while buildings, relatively static artifacts, are rooted in place. Ships are larger than most buildings and generally dynamic. It is too easy to dismiss these examples as having no relevance for architecture, which is fixed to the ground and custom crafted in the field rather than factory produced. There are lessons that can be examined and transferred from our sister industries to architecture. These lessons are not about outward form, style, or appearance. They are about processes and materials developed over the past decade that have overturned the ancient equilibrium between expenditure of resources and acquisition of benefits. The answer lies first in the emergence of the process engineer, the designer of methods.

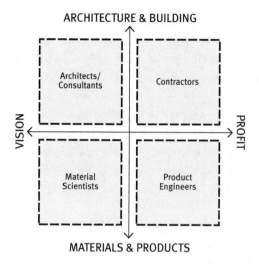

THE STRATIFICATION AND SEGREGATION OF ARCHITECTURE *Current architectural production is typified by stratification of the various components used in designing and implementing a building. As a result, the corresponding disciplines that are responsible for each segregate themselves within the stratified field. There is total self-segregation and no collective intelligence.*

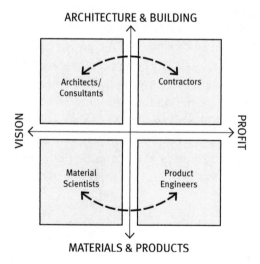

LIMITED COMMUNICATION *There is very little communication in the architectural model between disciplines. What communication does exist is not a true communicative relationship, but rather a hierarchical one in which one party is hired by the other to fulfill a particular role, such as a lighting consultant providing the lighting scheme for an architect.*

1.5   INTEGRATION, NOT SEGREGATION

The first act of design in this world beyond the old equilibrium is the redesign of the relations among those responsible for the making of things. The single most devastating consequence of modernism has been the embrace of a process that segregates designers from makers: The architect has been separated from the contractor, and the materials scientist has been isolated from the product engineer.

The automotive, shipbuilding, and aircraft industries, however, have developed models of engagement that integrate all acts of design and production. Their design departments and production departments have ceased to exist as independent entities within large organizations. Designers and producers are members of a team that comes together to solve specific problems.

The process of making is no longer entirely linear.

Producers engage in design, and designers engage in production. Production becomes part of the design process by working with assemblers from the outset; designers picture how things are made, their sequence of assembly, and their joining systems. Materials scientists are drawn into direct conversation and problem-solving with product engineers and even with designers. The intelligence of all relevant disciplines is used as a collective source of inspiration and constraint.

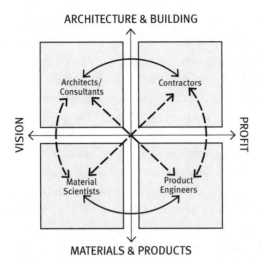

BREAKING OUT OF THE BOX *The four major disciplines need to cross the boundaries established by their traditional roles. All parties must seek a balance between vision and profit. There need to be reciprocal relationships between the developers of materials and products with the implementers and appliers.*

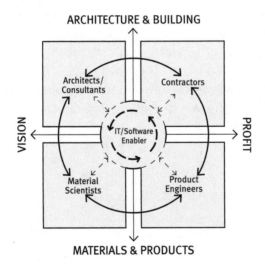

ENABLING COLLECTIVE INTELLIGENCE *An entire new industry that produces communication/collaboration software has made it possible for the various parties involved in a project to have realtime sharing of information. This instantaneous communication allows each party to be aware and involved with the other various disciplines throughout the entire process of a project.*

1.6   TOOLS OF THE PROCESS ENGINEER

The charts that govern the levels of responsibility for making decisions about design in the production of most complex artifacts have
in the past been largely hierarchical and top-down, a centralized
network. Most actual production has been equally hierarchical, but
with the sequence inverted, from the bottom up. Gravity has generally governed the physical sequence of production. Be it ship, car,
plane, or building, each began from the ground then extended up
into a frame that would be sequentially infilled and sheathed, part-
by-part, within the completely erected frame.

The physical process—like the decision-making structure—was hierarchical, since the entire framework, from the subsurface up, was
erected first, then systems were coursed through the structure, from
their source to the most remote points of distribution. Finally, walls
were installed and finishes applied. While many activities over-
lapped, with some beginning while others concluded, the actual
production process remained largely hierarchical.

**The process engineer today thrives on the fundamentally chaotic
nature of most forms of complex design and production.**

There is no need to force designing and making into straightjackets.
Designing need not be controlled entirely from the top down and
making need not proceed sequentially from the bottom up.
Problems can be separated into small pieces and solved both individually and together.

It is the process engineer who makes this possible through the
design of interactive tools that today are no longer physical but virtual. They are the tools of information and communication. The
process is set up to solve problems in the broadest way possible
through immediate visualization and interaction.

Airplanes

Ships

Cars

INDUSTRIES WITH INTEGRATED COLLABORATION

PUTTING THE PARADIGM TO THE TEST *Other major industries have already implemented the tools of the new collective intelligence paradigm. They have proven that connectivity Web sites and enabling software aid in speeding up the process of development, while increasing quality and reducing cost. (Images: courtesy Boeing, Kvaerner Philadelphia Shipyard Inc., Magna Steyr.)*

1.7   AN EXAMPLE: THE CAR

In the manufacture of automobiles, the linear addition of parts along the main assembly line that once produced the Model T has, in recent years, been replaced by the production of integrated modules, each composed of hundreds of parts and provided by a number of different suppliers.

Oddly enough, we become better at assembling and integrating by first disintegrating.

At Daimler/Chrysler, a process engineer divides the car to be produced into constituent *chunks*, or modules. The car today only becomes whole at the end of the manufacturing process, in those minutes of final assembly. Along the way, it is today designed and produced in independent chunks. Design and production teams are assembled at the outset to develop and produce each chunk. These teams are drawn from many organizations that begin with the OEM (original equipment manufacturer, in this case Daimler/Chrysler) and extend far into the supply chain. Product engineers and materials scientists from suppliers converge with designers, human-factors engineers, and production-line employees and supervisors to develop each chunk. Some of the principal chunks of a car are front fascia (grille, headlights) bars, and chrome strips; front suspension systems and steering; engine compartment (includes submodules); cockpit and instrument panels (sometimes includes steering column); seats; headliner (includes visors and electronics); carpet (molded to fit); tire and wheel assemblies; fuel system and tank; doors; stamping from body shop (includes front and rear floor, doors, hood, deck lid, fenders).

Each chunk is composed of many parts that are preassembled off the main assembly line, either in an adjoining facility, in a nearby plant, or at a remote location. Every part, right down to each individual screw, is defined and controlled by a three-dimensional process sheet that details all features and installation procedures. Design

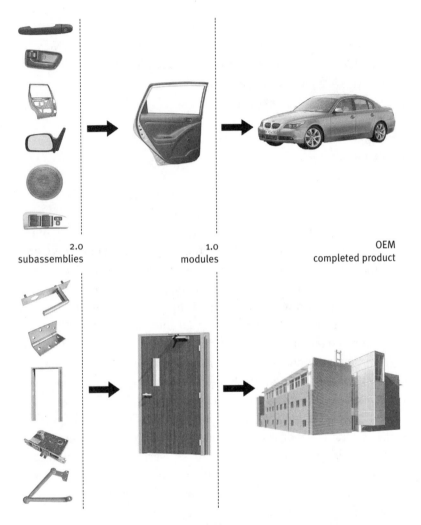

2.0
subassemblies

1.0
modules

OEM
completed product

Q = INTEGRATED COMPONENT CONSTRUCTION

IMPROVING THE SUPPLY CHAIN *The automotive industry has determined that expanding the supply chain into a few tiers has improved the quality of the final product and reduced its cost. Instead of having all parts arrive at the final point of assembly, the tiers gradually build up collections of parts to supply modules or integrated component assemblies to the original equipment manufacturer.*

aids, usually actual photographs of the assembly process, are developed. The *chunk teams* adjust the modules for manufacturing and installation. Quality gates all along the way require certification before development and production can proceed to the next stage.

The entire process is controlled electronically through direct links among all participants, from the OEM to the suppliers, and installed on the assembly line. Individual parts and modules are barcoded to enable instant tracking and to ensure that each is installed in the proper module or vehicle. If the wrong part is installed, warnings sound.

mid 1990's

goal
concept definition | concept development | series and production development | pilot

gateway
confirm vision | agree on goals | confirm concept | functional verification | product verification | ramp up

phase

|←------package development------→|

|←-------------skin styling-------------→|

|←---------------structure design and engineering---------------→|

     |←--semi-prototypes--→|

         |←-------first prototypes-------→|

                 |←-------second prototypes-------→|

         |←--------------------vehicle testing---------------------→|

month 0   month 58

VS.

present day

goal
building phase | concept | series and production development

gateway
confirm vis. | goals | concept | functional verif. | product verif. | ramp up

phase

|←--package development--→|

|←------skin styling-----→|

|←--simulations, digital mock-ups, digital assembly--→|

               |←-first prototypes-→|

|←--------------vehicle testing--------------------→|

month 0   month 38   month 58

T = TIME FROM CONCEPTION TO MARKET

REDUCING DESIGN AND CONSTRUCTION TIME *Digital modeling, virtual testing, supply-chain management, and corporate in-house connectivity are just a few of the process improvements made by the auto industry to dramatically reduce the time from conception to market of a vehicle. (Source: "BMW AG: The Digital Auto Project A," 1998, President/Fellows of Harvard College.)*

1.8   RESULTS: HIGHER QUALITY, MORE SCOPE AND FEATURES, LESS TIME, LOWER COST

Each module comes to the main plant complete and ready to be attached quickly to the vehicle. The various modules that form a car are designed and produced in parallel, drastically reducing the overall time-to-market for the complete car. Since each supplier is a discrete entity that has its full resources trained both on the problem of designing and producing a module whose component subassemblies fit together precisely and on optimizing the attention paid to the user's needs, that module has a markedly higher probability of achieving elevated quality and enhanced features. In addition, since quality control is introduced at the level of each type of module, the quality of the manufactured modules is further enhanced. The time and total cost of labor required to install modules at the point of final assembly are dramatically reduced. Thus the total time and cost for the car overall are reduced, as are the quantities and costs of material.

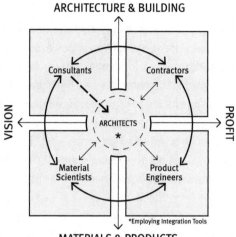

ARCHITECTURE & BUILDING

VISION ← → PROFIT

*Employing Integration Tools

MATERIALS & PRODUCTS

MANAGING INTELLIGENCE *Architects will serve as the overseers of the exchange of information. They will orchestrate the interactions and prompt the disciplines to work together. This role is not advocacy of the architect as a master builder, but rather as a twenty-first century maestro.*

1.9 MASTER BUILDING

The mandate. The processes. The materials. The information tools. All are present today in ways that have not coalesced in high architecture since the early Renaissance. Our market—the clients who build and the users who inhabit a building—have seen and reaped the benefits of redesigned methods and processes in other industries. Increasingly, they are demanding similar progress in architecture. We can no longer claim exclusion on the basis of attachment to the ground and customized design and construction.

The claim of exclusion risks irrelevance for architects.

New processes offer elevation of the art of architecture: more control, higher quality, and improved features. To do so, we must look deeper into what lies beyond mere appearances—to see how we do things, not merely what they look like. Gravity and hierarchy no longer dictate all processes. We must forge general and project-based relations with those whom architecture has in the past avoided, not only contractors, but also product engineers and materials scientists.

Here, at the turn of the twenty-first century, there has been an exponential explosion in the creation of new materials, unlike any in history. Relatively few of these materials have yet made their way into architecture, but many are now used in other industries, where they have allowed important gains in quality and features. We must overcome an industrywide aversion to research and experimentation in order to speed the integration of these new materials into architecture.

Lacking at the start of the twentieth century was the information needed to effect real change in the way we build. Tools to represent and transfer information instantly and completely are with us today. They allow connections among research, design, depiction, and making that have not existed since specialization began during the Renaissance.

II

ROLE REMINDERS IN THE NEW WORLD

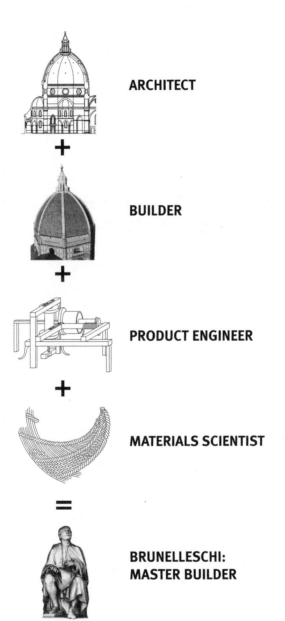

ARCHITECT

+

BUILDER

+

PRODUCT ENGINEER

+

MATERIALS SCIENTIST

=

**BRUNELLESCHI:
MASTER BUILDER**

MASTER OF ALL TRADES   *The Renaissance afforded Filippo Brunelleschi the opportunity to be a master builder due to the relative simplicity of building technologies of the time.*

2.1   THE ARCHITECT: THE MASTER BUILDER

The architect forms a shelter out of an idea about use; subdivides the space and develops a plan for relations among assemblies, then works with the assembler, the contractor, to develop joinery systems that unite the assemblies into a whole.

When the aspiration pushes beyond simple utility of building to architecture, it is the architect who pushes the assemblies and their joints by massing, shaping, surfacing, and profiling.

The master builder was a person who combined the roles of architect, builder, engineer, and scientist. Most buildings, both modest and aspiring, were designed and erected by master builders until only a few hundred years ago.

Filippo Brunelleschi was such a man. He had nearly total personal control and responsibility for the making of the dome of S. Maria del Fiore in Florence. He was the architect, builder, engineer, and scientist. In the course of the dome's construction, his innovations cut across all four disciplines. The dome was an architectural triumph. Its segmentation, exposed ribs, scale, proportion, and its air of lightness that lift it above the city continue to delight.

The construction of the dome required the invention of new lifts, including an ingenious and unprecedented screw jack. The structural integrity of the dome relies in part on new uses of old products, in this case, brick deployed in a spiral configuration and iron used to reinforce the drum. Brunelleschi was an innovative architect, builder, product engineer, and materials scientist.

The role of master builder has today both contracted and splintered. Design-builders (note that the term is not architect-builders) are just that: they design and they build. In no way do they aspire to master building.

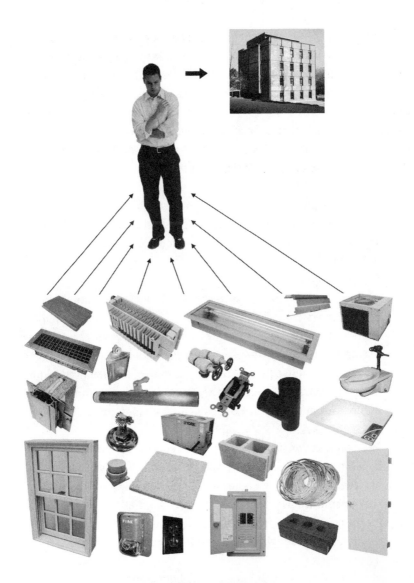

MASTER CONTROLLER

LOSING CONTROL   *The last century witnessed an unprecedented development of new materials and improved environmental systems, as well as a new understanding of old topics, such as acoustics. This expansion of choices has added up to infinitely more complex and specialized buildings that require expertise in more subjects than one architect can master. The architect cnow coordinates the many diverse consultants who are able to master their own specialties.*

Design-builders work in the segments of the market that are driven by low cost and fast schedule. They select from the building products available but do not push product engineering, and they probably have never even thought about materials science. Their artifacts are buildings, not architecture. At the same time, the segments of the market that care about quality have been served by the combined industry of highly discrete professions: architect, builder, engineer, and scientist, each of whom functions within a separate organization that has its own distinct agenda and aspirations.

No architects today think of themselves as master builders. The disjunction of the various elements of master building has been institutionalized over the past few centuries by means of separate educational programs, separate licensing and insurance requirements, and separate professional organizations. Further, the industrialization of the production of most building material in the developed world has removed product engineering from the purview of the architect. The aggregation of environmental control systems in architecture hammered the final nail in the coffin of master building. Most buildings are no longer simple vessels, shells formed around a use, but machines of enormous complexity, coursed through by numerous systems that control the environment of its interior and connect it to the external world.

Architecture requires control, deep control, not merely of an idea, but also of the stuff we use to give form to the idea.

The architect has been much diminished in the now centuries-old splintering and segregation of the former role of the master builder. Ironically, by narrowing its realm of significant interest to appearance only, architecture sacrificed control of its one remaining stronghold: appearance.

The architect makes architecture in equal measure with ideas and materials. Architecture is conceived out of ideas about site and use,

ARCHITECT'S CURRENT SOURCE FOR COMPONENTS

DESIGN BY CATALOG   *The ever-increasing knowledge required to master all of the specialities associated with buildings have relegated architects to an administrative role, in which they must choose from what is available and do little development of their own materials and products.*

ideas that are shaped and reshaped into form to suit purpose and place. Materials, the stuff we build with, give physical substance to this shape and to the idea that animates it.

By allowing architecture to become reduced to the current degree and by relinquishing responsibility for assembly, product development, and materials science to specialists, the architect has allowed the means and methods of building to move outside the sphere of architecture.

It is the builder who now decides how the building will be assembled—the means, method, and sequence of assembly—all of which affect form. The product engineer, through control of the marketplace of manufactured building materials, now decides what products are available for use. The materials scientist, for his part, now decides upon the composition, the physical substance, of those products. This splintering of architecture into segregated specialties has been disastrous. Once, there was a seamless integration of the constituent elements of building through the person of the master builder, who had control over the materials, products, and construction of architecture. Today, there is little interaction among these disciplines, particularly between architect and builder on the one hand and product engineer and materials scientist on the other.

The role of the architect in this evolving world of construction processes remains squarely centered on an architecture formed about an idea of use and place, but we must also have tentacles extended deep into assembly, products, and materials. While we cannot return to the idea of the master builder embodied in a single person, the architect can force the integration of the several spun-off disciplines of architecture—construction, product engineering, and materials science—all with the aim of reuniting substance with intent.

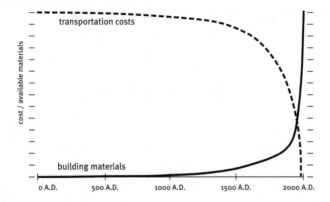

THE AGE OF EXPLORATION *For several millennia, the methods and materials of construction were relatively limited. Local materials readily found in nature were the norm. In the midnineteenth century, however, technological developments in transportation and materials science expanded the available choices exponentially.*

2.2   **THE MATERIAL SCIENTIST: PURPOSE, NOT STYLE**

To take advantage of the current explosion in the creation of new materials, the materials scientists who develop the materials used in building and architecture must expand their realm of interest into architecture. These scientists test, record, and publish data about the properties of materials. They assess risk and validate use. The scientists who work with new building materials are currently so remote from the architect and contractor they serve that they might just as well be working at another, altogether different endeavor. Ask materials scientists if they have ever spoken with an architect or contractor about product development. Or ask architects and engineers if they have ever had a conversation about the stuff, the substance, of our buildings with a materials scientist. The answer will almost certainly be no. What can the materials scientist contribute to the development of a new architecture that works toward the integration of information and materials? Why is the establishment of this cross-discipline dialogue so critical now at the beginning of the twenty-first century?

The products used in construction changed little until the middle of the nineteenth century. For the most part, the selection of materials was limited to substances readily available in nature: stone, wood, straws and grasses, masonry, concrete, and basic metals. While some chemical transformations of these raw materials, such as the formation of brick and tile from clay, and of concrete from cement, lime, and aggregate, have been known and developed for thousands of years, there were relatively few such transforming combinations in use before the middle of the nineteenth century. Further, because transportation was difficult and expensive, most products were likely to come from locations near the construction site. As a result, exotic materials from far-away locations were rarely used.

In the second half of the nineteenth century, there was an explosion in the development of new materials that became an important agent of change in architecture and construction. Materials and

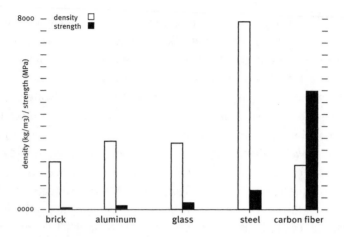

PERFORMANCE EVOLUTION *New materials are constantly being developed that outperform those traditionally used in building. Unfortunately, the use of new materials in architecture often overlooks the performance data and chooses a product merely for its novel stylistic value.*

composites developed during this period almost always required considerable transformation and processing. Examples include steel and reinforced concrete.

The development of new materials has been exponentially vaster in quantity and type than at any preceding time, and the pace of invention continues to accelerate. Whole new categories of material have been invented: polyaramids such as Kevlar, Goretex, and ETFE; foamed materials that range from polyurethane to metal and many new adhesives. Other categories have been transformed and expanded: ceramics, aluminum, and titanium. A vast new field of composites, born of the purposeful combination of previously separate materials, lies before us: reinforced plastics; polymers threaded with glass fiber, aramids, or carbon, and thin films applied to fabrics.

There are good reasons to develop and use these materials that have nothing to do with novelty, although that seems to be the motivating factor for the use of most materials today.

The use of new materials in architecture is today rarely more than a stylistic statement made in an effort to claim modernity merely through the use of an innovative product. Novelty alone, however, cannot sustain use.

These new materials deserve further research, development, and exploitation because they hold out the promise of greater quality and new features combined with less time to fabricate and a reduction in the cost of the products they form. Examples of purposeful new uses abound in the auto and aircraft industries. Delphi Systems, for example, has a new product to support an automotive cockpit. The purpose of any cockpit support is twofold: to provide an armature to which cockpit features are attached and to increase personal safety by maintaining the integrity of the passenger compart-

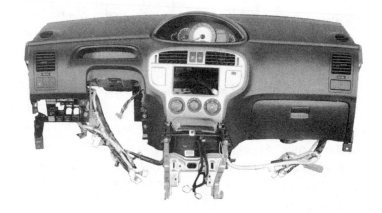

INTELLIGENT INNOVATION *The Delphi Systems cockpit provides an armature to support cockpit features, which increases personal safety by maintaining the integrity of the passenger compartment in the event of a crash, and is used as a duct to distribute air. This innovation eliminates several parts that formerly served the same functions. (Image: courtesy Delphi Corporation.)*

ment in the event of a crash. Delphi's new support performs both these functions better than the supports currently used in the rest of the industry. It is a fiber-reinforced plastic tube that is both stronger and lighter than its steel predecessor. Furthermore, it performs a third function: it is also used as a duct to distribute air to the passenger compartment, thus eliminating several additional parts. This innovative use of a new material results in an increase in quality and features through the use of fewer joints and parts and also in a reduction in cost and the time required for assembly.

Boeing designers and engineers are also engaged in exploiting the possibilities of new materials, particularly through the company's Monolithic Design Initiative that aims to reduce the total number of parts in a plane. The aim of this initiative is to produce planes of higher quality in less time at lower cost. A central tactic of Boeing in this initiative is the use of new materials that allow the formation of one part from what, in the past, would have been many.

The integration of materials scientists and product engineers into the process of building design would be a start toward the exploitation of purposeful innovations in the materials used in architecture.

While a few innovative materials have gained widespread use in architecture, most materials technologies have been slow to penetrate contemporary construction practices. The reasons are many and include the cost of testing and the exposure to liability inherent in new materials. Just as important, however, is the lack of vision on the part of architects, contractors, and product engineers that is necessary to lead the way to substantive new uses.

VS.

FROM PRIMITIVE HUT TO HIERARCHICAL LIBRARY   *The myriad components used in a building today require a comprehensive catalog that orders elements based upon their function and materials. The dominant ordering system, CSI, uses a 16-division, 16-volume set to allow efficient access to these products. (Image: University of Pennsylvania Rare Book and Manuscript Library.)*

2.3   THE PRODUCT ENGINEER: REPACKAGING
THE PARTS OF ARCHITECTURE

The product engineer locates, exploits, and transfers materials from one realm to another to apply them to new uses in building and architecture from earlier uses in other fields, such as product design, shipbuilding, car manufacturing, and aircraft production. These engineers transform discrete building materials into integrated components that combine several functions and materials into a single element for final assembly. The product engineer is the interlocutor between the architect and the materials.

Vernacular construction uses what is immediately at hand. Time itself, through trial and error and the handing down of traditions of craft across generations, is the product engineer in this world. Today, most architecture in the developed world requires at least some products that are not immediately at hand. These are products extracted from nature, often at remote locations, which are then reconstituted for use in building.

The product engineer develops these architectural commodities for companies that manufacture and distribute them. The Construction Specification Institute (CSI) assists the product engineer by placing the new product in its informational hierarchy. CSI has organized the vast mosaic of the thousands of commodities available into 16 divisions that are based on a combination of function and material.

Information systems, such as the one set up by CSI, order facts in ways that allow efficient access. The danger in any such framework, however, is that the information system itself takes on the guise of reality. This is, in fact, what has happened with the way we order the products we use in building. The 16 divisions of the currently dominant information system contribute to sustaining a reality that is no longer productive.

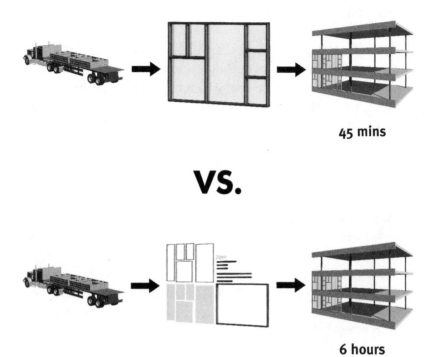

45 mins

VS.

6 hours

RETHINKING PROCESS   *The traditional building paradigm is to gather all of the parts of a building at the site and then assemble them piece by piece. This process leads product engineers to think in a piecemeal manner when designing building products. If we were to construct our buildings on site utilizing preassembled components, the engineers could think in a more effective wholistic part-to-whole manner.*

The CSI informational structure fragments the work of the product engineer into thousands of competing independent products. At times, this hierarchy becomes self-defeating, as when the same product is relevant to many product categories. Rather than looking for 10 solutions to a problem, the designer must look for thousands of solutions. Innovation resides primarily at the level of individual products and materials, not in the seams in between. CSI does not have a way of categorizing products and materials that solve a variety of problems. It is these seams, however, that dictate the degree of quality, the duration of construction, and the level of cost that constrain all that we do. It is also these seams that show the opportunities that lie ahead.

The product engineer needs to take the blinders off and focus on permutations of elements rather than on single parts and separate materials.

A vital new responsibility of the product engineer is the development of integrated component assemblies—modules, chunks, grand blocks—that cut across all the separate categories of material and function.

The product engineer can lead the way in rewriting the specifications in the information system that pertain to integrated component assemblies. Parts need to become combinations that can cut across several current CSI categories. We need a new *Sweets Catalog* for integrated components. The information system needs to enable, not restrain, integration, and the product engineer needs to work broadly and collaboratively in order to effect the integration of various disciplines.

1913   **2001**

STUCK ON THE ASSEMBLY LINE *The current building process is akin to the original Ford assembly line. Parts are gathered and delivered to the site, where they are placed in turn in their proper location on the chassis. It is a fully linear and hierarchical process. (Images: from the collections of Henry Ford Museum & Greenfield Village.)*

2.4   THE CONTRACTOR: RESURRECTING THE CRAFT OF ASSEMBLY

In all but the smallest of buildings, the contractor today is often no more than a purchasing agent. Few actually build. The role of the contractor is to buy the parts of the building, then to oversee the installation of those parts in accordance with the requirements of the contract.

The contractor of tomorrow works in the seams between the product engineer and the architect where the craft and quality of joinery reside. The contractor—the assembler, the collector—accumulates the parts and strives to minimize the amount of field assembly by employing to the greatest extent possible off-site fabrication in factories dedicated to the development of integrated component assemblies.

_____

In this sense, larger building contractors, at least in the United States, resemble the original equipment manufacturer, the oems of the automotive world.

Today, the larger contractors, like automotive OEMS, subcontract most of the segments of their product to other, more specialized builders or manufacturers. Each has forgone the traditional craft of making by relying on the contemporary process of assembly.

The building contractor and the automotive OEM have never been further removed from actual production than they are today. There is even talk in the auto industry that some OEMS will simply become brand managers and that the entire automobile will be built under subcontract to another entity engaged solely in manufacturing.

Here, however, the parallels between automobiles and architecture end. In the making of automobiles, all is not lost in this new world of assembly. In the auto, and to a lesser extent in the shipbuilding and aircraft industries, the prospects for quality in design and con-

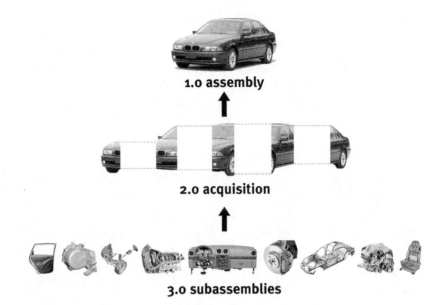

1.0 assembly

2.0 acquisition

3.0 subassemblies

THE MULTITIERED MODULE SUPPLY CHAIN   *If architecture were to incorporate the supply chain model of the automobile industry, the contractor would assume the role of assembler acting as an oem, such as BMW, Ford, Volkswagen, etc.*

struction—for a return to craft—have, ironically, increased by the splintering of responsibility. As initially conceived and built in the nineteenth century, cars were relatively simple machines that were custom crafted one by one, and had relatively few parts and systems. In 1907, Ford standardized production for the mass market by using the assembly line, a transforming innovation in which the artifact moves to the specialized worker rather than the worker to specified areas of the artifact.

Initially, the car itself was simplified as mass-production strategies relentlessly pursued the lowest cost and the largest market. This reductive strategy, however, did not last long. The customer soon began to demand variation and enhancements. As year by year, system after system was added to a car, the total number of parts and the complexity of their relations increased to the point where the centralization of design and production began to compromise, rather than enhance, its quality. Today, cars have simply become too complex and their various systems too specialized to be designed, managed, and produced by single entities. In response to economic pressures, the auto industry has taken advantage of the production economies offered by contemporary techniques and has dismantled its centralized command-and-control procedures in favor of the segmentation of production. Design and production have been segmented and reassigned to a few integrated component assemblies that produce modules or chunks of the entire product.

With this fragmentation, the focus of both design and production has sharpened, quality has increased, and the cost and time of production have decreased.

What does this make of the OEMS? They become assemblers. Their focus is no longer on the piece-by-piece construction of a car that today is composed of approximately 4,000 individual parts. Most fabrication now occurs off site in factories dedicated to the produc-

VS.

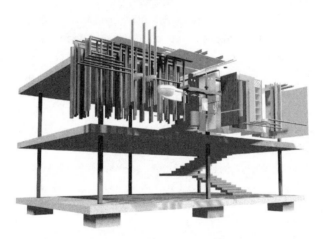

THE BENEFIT OF PREPACKAGING *The true potential of Le Corbusier's Maison Domino as a frame-work for mass production would finally be achieved through the use of integrated component assemblies.*

tion of integrated component assemblies in the form of modules or chunks. The OEM can concentrate on the integration and assembly of a far more manageable number of components. Assembly evolves to a higher level of craft than was possible with the old piece-by-piece method of acquisition and building.

Compared to OEMs in the automotive world, building contractors, as well as architects and product engineers, are still in the nineteenth century. Buildings continue to be assembled largely piece by piece in the field, in much the same way that the car was put together before the advent of mass production. Where is the evolution in building construction? Why is it that large parts of our buildings are not assembled as fully integrated major components, off site, in controlled factory conditions? Were this to be the norm rather than the exception, the building contractor, like the OEM, would become an assembler, liberated to concentrate on quality and speed.

The craft, quality, and speed of joinery would become art once more.

The contractor, as an assembler, would work between the architect and the product engineer to develop integrated component assemblies that would repackage the elements of construction into a vastly smaller number of components ready for final field assembly.

III

ENABLING SYSTEMS AS REGULATORY STRUCTURE

 **VS.**

REGULATING LINES VERSUS SUPPLY CHAINS   *Control has always been a goal of the architect. Control was sought through various mathematical schemes, systems of proportion or modular relationships. Today, control is achieved through the use of information science. The architect must seek control through supply-chain management and product development, rather than through formal exercises of geometry. (Image: 2003 Artists Rights Society, New York/ADAGP, Paris/FLC.)*

3.1 ENABLING COMMUNICATIONS

Information management used as a regulatory system allows design and construction to acknowledge what they really are—organized chaos. It is a regulatory system that would not force architecture and construction into today's straightjacket of hierarchical, top-to-bottom practice in design and construction.

There is no single mathematical construct, no modular or classical system of proportions and relationships that is either necessary or desirable for control and order in this new world of architecture. Geometry is now only one small facet of a far more vast regulatory structure that is grounded in information science.

The regulating lines of an information management system are the new Modulor.

The development of this fully integrated web of tools to conceive and manage architecture will be the enabling structure, the new Modulor of this twenty-first century way of making. The results will not be sameness but differences. There will be no types.

We need more information in order to expand the various objects we produce, to save us from a production reduced to a limited set of object types. We need more information if we are to conceive components, wholly and fully in the round, that are developed in different places by different designers. We need more information to enhance the speed and comprehensiveness of our conceptions. We need more information early on in the process of conception in order to project cost, method, and sequence of assembly into our design considerations so that they will act as positive constraints that make our design solutions powerful because they are lean. We need more information to locate all the pieces that make up the components of our buildings throughout the process of design, fabrication, and assembly. We need more information to know immediately when a component has been improperly installed. The development of such a fully integrated web of informational tools to conceive a building and manage its design is the regulating and enabling structure, the new Modulor of this new way of making.

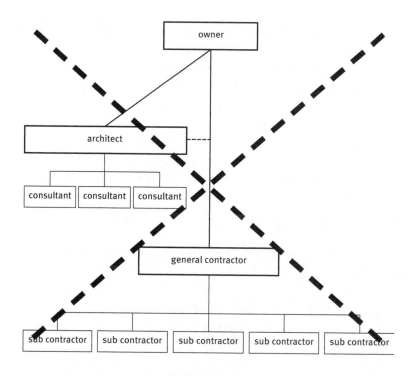

CONCEPTION

THE MYTH OF CONTROL   *The AIA Owner-Architect organizational hierarchy chart is a purely pro-
motional device. Rarely do the illustrated positions of control ever hold true, especially if a result
of good architecture is desired.*

The making of architecture is an act of organized chaos. This will not be a happy revelation to the buying public. If the real nature of the process were ever conveyed to the client, the architect's reward for honesty would be a lack of work. Instead, the architect places before the client a diagram of organizational structure that is a powerful marketing device to suggest that everything is under control.

The usual organizational charts for making a building depict a thoroughly hierarchical process in which chains of command extend in lock-step order from top to bottom. These diagrams are of two types. The first, drawn up for comfort during conception and programming, shows the client at the top, seemingly in a position of control. The architect is below, taking direction from the client, and various specialty engineers and consultants are in turn further below, receiving their direction from the architect.

As architecture moves from conception to realization, a second diagram supplants the first to show the contractor now moving into the level directly below the owner. In the owner's interest, the architect is now an advisor who has specific rights and responsibilities.

_____

The reality of making architecture is far more complex than any diagram can convey.

To start with, most clients are far from monolithic single entities. Rather than a single group organized in a command-and-control hierarchy, there might be dozens of individuals and organizations within a client group. Each individual or group can affect the outcome at almost any time and drive the solution in unpredictable directions.

A second blow to any diagram of hierarchical control comes from the design side of the process. Each new system added to architecture over the past 150 years has brought additional consultants, engineers, and specialists who develop, design, and manage the integration of each system into the practice of architecture.

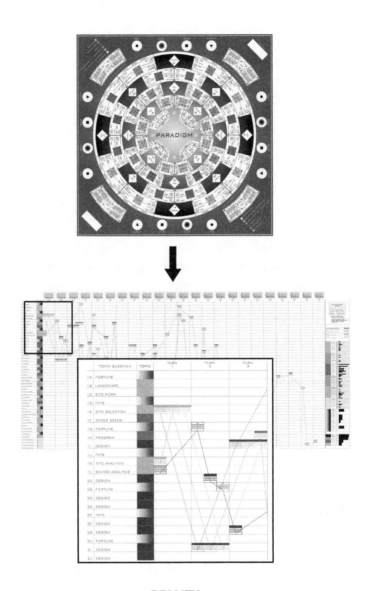

REALITY

THE CHAOS OF REALITY   The current act of building is a truly chaotic process confined to linear and pseudohierarchical systems. The above illustrated board game, Paradigm, developed by University of Pennsylvania Master of Architecture student J. Timothy McCarthy, accepts this chaos and anticipates the evolution of the design and construction process by favoring nonhierarchical and nonlinear gaming strategies. (Images: J.Timothy McCarthy.)

All these systems compete for the same limited space, and although two-dimensional coordination drawings attempt to identify and solve some of the problems of integrating these systems, the conflicting realities are most often worked out in the field, where the construction in progress serves as the mock-up. A third attack on the neat hierarchical chart comes from the hundreds of suppliers of parts and components, each one of whom is responsible to dozens of subcontractors for the majority of the detailed design and implementation required by each part or component. Each of these suppliers may also be responsible for supplying the materials used to build hundreds, even thousands, of simultaneous projects. Suppliers interact with design and construction in ways that are also often unpredictable. Competing work, inherent labor shortages, strikes, and the logistics of supplying and transporting raw materials are but a few of the many variables that are far removed from the control of the owner and architect yet can affect entire sequences of construction and the final outcome in chaotic ways.

Architecture is not alone in having to face up to the reality of the chaos out of which it develops.

Business management consultants, working with all types of corporations and governments, are coming to believe that a hierarchical method of command and control rarely parallels reality. Instead of insisting on hierarchy, these consultants and the executives they advise are coming to accept chaos as inevitable and working to understand, appreciate, and organize complexity. Rather than attempt to force all problem-solving to proceed from the top down or to undergo review only from the bottom up, new management theories suggest that large-scale problems can be most effectively solved by being taken apart and solved as smaller problems, each of which demands distinct responsibilities and authorities. The results are then patched together, and considerable attention is given to the seams conjoining the several solutions.

SEQUENTIAL

VS.

SIMULTANEOUS

FRAMING VERSUS QUILTING   *Framing is the old way of making in architecture, in which hierarchical parts are sequentially aggregated into a whole. Quilting is the new way of making in architecture, in which integrated assemblies are elements that can be made in various locations by various makers and integrated seamlessly with the other assemblies to form the whole. (Images: Hulton-Deutsch Collection/Corbis, Ted Streshinsky/Corbis.)*

As in business and manufacturing, the acceptance of chaos in the conception and construction of architecture requires certain beliefs and strategies. If hierarchical command-and-control models no longer match present-day realities, then the theories we use to understand, organize, and interact with those realities must change. Chaos can no longer be controlled in classical terms from detail to whole and from whole to detail. There can no longer be completely consistent ascending and descending orders through which parts are aggregated into wholes and wholes are disassembled into parts. What we can have, however, are integrated components, elements of solutions made in different locations by different entities, that are integrated seamlessly through the agency of information management.

This difference between ways of making is evident in the difference between ways of framing and quilting. Framing is entirely gravity-based. The frame must be present before anything else can be placed. It is a precondition.

Quilting, by contrast to framing, requires only a conceptual, not a physical, framework.

Once the conceptual system exists, the elements of the quilt—the patches—can be fabricated in any order and assembled, that is, sewn together in any number of permutations. With a simple set of rules about size, and perhaps theme, color, and pattern, small groups or individuals can design and make pieces of an artifact relatively independently of each other. When the pieces are complete, the makers come together as assemblers, for a brief time, in the ritual quilting bee, an exercise in communal patchwork. Things that were once separate are sewn together into a new whole. The same process holds true for complex management problems and buildings. Both can be broken apart into pieces, these pieces solved, and then joined into an integrated whole. Patching together the solutions to smaller problems into a larger solution can be an effective way to generate sound complex wholes.

PREVIOUS   **CURRENT**

NEW TOOLS, SAME PRODUCT *The architecture industry's move from T-square and linen to computer as a means of documentation has essentially been only a switch in media. The potential to
solid model with a computer has not been adopted, rather architects still use the computer for 2-
D drafting and "movie-set" 3-D representations.*

3.2 REPRESENTATION VERSUS SIMULATION

The information management tools we need in order to manage our chaos have already been developed in other industries. Deep within the world's largest building volume toil Boeing design and production engineers who use tools to design and produce aircraft that we could use in architecture.

In the aerospace industry individual aircraft lead parallel existences. Each aircraft is at once both virtual and actual. Each becomes complete first as fully modeled, attribute-laden information. Each aircraft is defined, then planned, bought, built, and supported throughout its life as an integrated information system. How is this different from architecture?

Buildings are represented; aircraft are modeled.

Representation is the art of defining one thing or person by use of another. The representation is a proxy, a stand-in for the original. Representation in production provides the information needed to build, but it is incomplete, segregated, and prone to inconsistency. Basic planning information in architecture remains today largely two-dimensional. This is especially true at the contractual level. Architecture relies upon flat projections to convey a construction: plans, sections, elevations, and details.

By contrast to representation, simulation is a complete three-dimensional regulatory structure. Simulation makes possible the fragmentation of large artifacts, such as aircraft, into large, integrated components that can be fabricated anywhere in the world and brought together for final assembly. Simulation is seamless and makes segregation possible. It gives us a whole model, complete down to the level of individual parts. All parts are known. All joints and corners are depicted. All can be seen from any point of view. Factors that constrain their design are embedded in the information supplied with individual parts. The maker of each part and its whereabouts in the chain of fabrication are known.

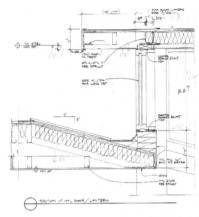 

BUILDING (representation)

VS.

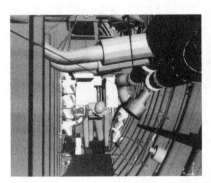 

AIRCRAFT (simulation)

PHYSICAL VERSUS VIRTUAL MOCK-UPS   *The great advantage the aerospace industry has over architecture is its use of solid modeling. With solid modeling, designers are able to produce a virtual mock-up of their entire product. A virtual mock-up allows them to test for critical performance criteria without having to invest time or resources in actually building anything. (Image: Boeing.)*

3.3   DESIGN TOOLS

By the use of simulation Boeing designers and engineers are able to take a virtual flight through a Boeing 777. A complete aircraft consisting of more than one million parts arrives on a screen. Through the agency of solid modeling, every part can be designed and envisioned both individually and in context, without the need for a physical mock-up. Parts of the design process, such as the routing of the hydraulic and electrical systems, that were once performed through extensive physical mock-ups are now developed electronically. Boeing engineers can simulate a view which moves from the skin of the aircraft, through the surface to a 5" by 6" shear-tie that fastens the exterior skin to the frame. They can view the process used to create this part, beginning with a wire frame then proceeding to the solid geometry. Point of view is no longer a limitation for Boeing. Every part comprising the overall aircraft is a solid that can be viewed from all points of view.

Unlike representation, simulation is not limited to a particular fixed point of view.

The properties of this shear-tie are fully embedded within the solid representation. Any dimension can be derived completely and accurately from the solid model, rendering the once necessary dimensional drawings now obsolete.

Additional dimensions, termed *effectivites* by Boeing designers, are added to images of each part. Effectivities are informational factors embedded within the depiction of individual parts to control their design. They identify the responsibilities of a part and record its placement in an individual aircraft. The effectivities also include property analyses that provide immediate physical information about the part: its weight, and the location of that weight within the aircraft, and its strength and resistance properties.

The bill of materials (BOM) is the informational mechanism that translates design into reality, image into construction. This is a critical

TRADITIONAL PAPER CHASE

VS.

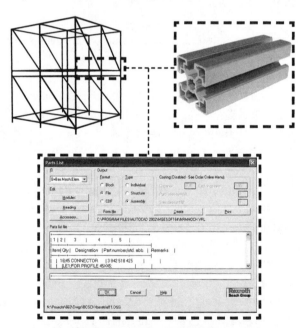

VIRTUALLY EMBEDDED

SMART DRAWINGS   *Software packages that integrate effectivities with models will eventually eliminate the inefficient and tedious conventional methods of documentation. All schedules and engineering data of an element will be available at the click of a button.*

tool, a present-day hammer that allows parts to be combined into modules and modules into an entire aircraft. One purpose of the BOM is to act as a guide to the location and properties of every *pure part*, or irreducible element that is joined to create each module of an aircraft. Each of these is recorded as a trace element through the agency of the BOM. The description, whereabouts, and status of any part or module can be instantaneously recovered. The BOM, which was a data management tool during design and fabrication, becomes a reference library of parts and the basic management tool throughout the service life of the aircraft. There are two seamless components of the BOM, an engineering bill of material (EBOM) and a manufacturing bill of material (MBOM). The EBOM is composed of design sheets that visually depict and numerically and verbally identify each individual part, and the MBOM organizes the parts identified in the EBOM into modules that are fully integrated collections of parts managed as a unit. At Boeing, an EBOM is compiled for each pure part. Without further manipulation, the EBOM would be composed of one million pure parts. Any tree created to suggest how the pure parts are related would be enormous and without hierarchy. Trunks, branches, and leaves would be indistinguishable from one another. There would, in fact, be no tree, only forest.

Boeing engineers have learned that in order to control cost it is necessary to modify the way assembly is managed. The tool they use to do this is the MBOM. The MBOM determines the assembly by managing its sequence. The cost of aircraft assembly is determined by the depth of the tree. The greater the number of levels to the tree, the higher the cost. A level is a collection of parts, an integrated component assembly. Modules are fully assembled collections of parts with some as large as an entire aircraft fuselage. They are fabricated elsewhere, sometimes nearby but often overseas, by subcontract to other entities. They arrive at the assembly plant for joining to other modules. The MBOM determines the sequence of joining and links individual products to time by specifying their date of arrival and installation at the assembly plant.

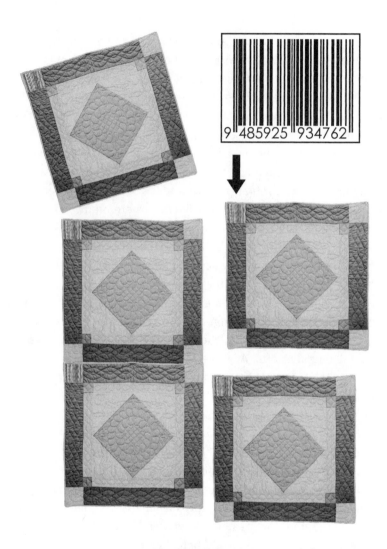

QUILT MANAGEMENT

THE CRITICAL WHOLE   *To work with a modular system or to use component assemblies, it is necessary to have a thorough understanding of the completed whole. A prevision of the final assembly and construction is the critical component that must occur as the originating act of the design process.*

The irony of modular assembly is that it places a premium on a complete understanding of the whole as a prerequisite to strategies for fragmentation. Visualization is regulatory structure. This visualization is like the vision of the quilt before it is sectioned. It is the common understanding among the participants in the creation of the artifact that allows craft to reemerge at the manageable level of individual sections. Simulation is the way we assure that the patching of the quilted sections into a unified whole—be it car, aircraft, ship, or building—joins and closes as craft.

In the manufacturing world, components are the patches.

In order to quilt you must first share. In quilting, the relation between the designer-fabricator and the patch is one-to-one. In the production of more complicated artifacts, many designers and fabricators, trained in different disciplines and located in different places, combine their individual talents and knowledge in creating each patch. What is the enabling mechanism for sharing the work that goes into the patches?

In manufacturing, sharing is done electronically. Each integrated EBOM and MBOM is shared, through secure server access, over the Internet in order to enable worldwide design and production at any time. Boeing engineers can work in tandem, leaving their day's design work open on an FTP (file transfer protocol) site so that their engineer and designer colleagues may open, use, save and exchange information with other corporate colleagues anywhere else. When the Boeing engineers return the next morning, their design work has been advanced through updated information from their suppliers and module assemblers.

In this new age of information exchange, the Modulor is organizationally enabled through shared software to exchange and manage design and information about cost, engineering, and quality at any moment of the day or night, every day of the year, everywhere around the world.

IV

PROCESSES WE DO NOT SEE

BLOCKS, CHUNKS, MODULES

DEFYING GRAVITY   The assembly of large objects used to be dictated by the laws of gravity. Building would typically start with a structural frame, proceed from the bottom, and move upwards hierarchically, adding elements until completion. Today, most of these industries have moved toward nongravity-based processes where pieces of the object are framed and outfitted independently of the whole and brought together only at final assembly. (Images: Kvaerner Philadelphia Shipyard Inc., Audi AG, Faurecia.)

4.1 GRAVITY, EVOLUTION, ECONOMICS

Underlying the new and emerging processes we do not see is a change in the way we address gravity in the assembly of large objects, be they ships, planes, cars or, by transfer, architecture. We do not often think of these large objects and buildings together. Ships, planes, and cars move a lot. Ideally buildings move very little. Yet all of these large objects have had this in common for most of their histories: They are all built from the bottom up. For each, gravity is the central force that draws all materials into a predictable hierarchical array about structural frames that are a precursor to all other elements, such as cladding, interiors, systems, and equipment. It is the unified structural frame, grounded to keel, chassis, or foundation, that counters gravity to lift and hold all later elements above water or ground. In a long-standing concession to gravity and its attendant difficulty of both fabricating and moving very large elements, most parts that go into the making of large things have historically arrived small—and numerous—at the point of final assembly, be it dry dock, factory, or building site. There are roughly 4,000 parts for a car, 1,000,000 parts for a Boeing 777, and millions for a large ship.

The process transformations that we do not see represent a profound change in the way we make large things.

The finished structure, be it ship, plane, or car, today counters gravity by eluding it during fabrication and reinstating it at final assembly. Makers no longer first frame the entire object. The ship, plane, and car are framed incrementally, and each increment is completely fitted out with systems, exteriors, and finishes, either in a remote location or near the site of final assembly, as grand blocks, modules, or chunks. Relatively few parts are installed during final assembly; most are completed elsewhere and transported to the construction site for joining to other grand blocks, modules, or chunks.

PART-BY-PART CONSTRUCTION

TRADITIONAL BUILDING   *Since the beginning of civilization, architecture has been built piece by piece. Parts are determined, gathered, and assembled. It is a fully linear process in which little trade-work can be done simultaneously. It is the way the pyramids were built and the way in which today's monuments are still being built. (Images: (middle) Bettmann/Corbis, (bottom) Zinat Yusufzai.)*

Keel-laying and groundbreaking are ancient origination rituals that have historically accompanied the start of construction for ships and buildings. The keel is the ship's symbolic and factual foundation. The keel is to the ship what the spine is to the body. It organizes all that is to follow, and the structural ribs that shape the ship's sides and deck are connected at the keel. We celebrate the laying of the keel because it marks the act of conception from which the rest of the ship evolves. The similar moment of origin for the construction of a building occurs at the symbolic breaking of the ground, the passage of a spade into the earth beneath the force of the makers' feet. The parting of earth allows the placement of foundations that root architecture to ground and support the frame or walls that organize all that is to come above.

Both keel-laying and groundbreaking symbolize a way of building that is as old as shipbuilding and architecture themselves. Each begins from the bottom, be it keel or foundation, then joins to it a supporting frame of ribs, either column or wall, then sheathes the structure in skin. Next follows the insertion of systems, interiors, and equipment to culminate in a completed ship or building. These acts have an order, a sequence to their hierarchy that has remained largely unchallenged throughout history. While there has always been some overlap between the end of one act of construction and the beginning of the next, the sequence of the acts in the plays of shipbuilding and architecture have remained the same: foundation, frame, skin, systems, finish, equipment.

AND

THE GOLIATH SCALE OF SHIPBUILDING

SIZE IS NOT AN ISSUE *The scale of shipbuilding is immense. Large grand blocks the size of a seven-story building are lifted by a goliath crane that moves them around as if they were toys. (Images: courtesy of Kvaerner Philadelphia Shipyard Inc.)*

4.2   SHIPBUILDING

The old Philadelphia Naval Base is not about urban blocks. It is about pieces, very large pieces, of ships: *grand blocks*. Three huge blue cranes—one a bar crane with the word "Kvaerner" painted across it—mark the site of a new enterprise within the former naval yards. A collection of underused, early twentieth-century brick structures buttress the site where the three cranes now distinguish the yard. The scale of these cranes is so vast, even against the backdrop of what we used to think of as very large decaying ships, sheds, and dry docks, that one immediately senses the presence of a new way of making, of change and promise within the ruins of a past long since overtaken by more productive worlds.

Ship construction today depends on a geographic idea about building, rather than on the systems-based idea of yesterday's shipbuilding.

A grand block is a completed segment of a ship that can range in weight from 150 to 1,000 tons. A grand block includes all the systems in a given segment of a ship, from its structure and outside hull to its inner hulls and all its machinery for heating, ventilating, air conditioning, plumbing, fire protection, electrical power and voice and data systems. It also includes all its program compartments and finishes, including painting inside and out. It is generally only as small as it needs to be in order to be built entirely inside a building, then moved out to the dry dock, lifted into position and welded to its companion grand blocks.

In the past, as in the contemporary construction of a building, there were overlaps between tasks in shipbuilding. For example, fitting out the interior and installing the systems in the bottom of the ship could begin before the top of the ship was completed. For the most part, however, the process, like the product, was literally an inverted hierarchy. Working from the bottom up, few trades could begin anything until most of the structure was well along. Structural work

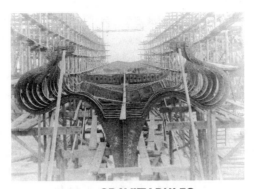

1910 - GRAVITY RULES

VS.

2001 - QUILTING RULES

BREAKING WITH TRADITION *The urgent demand for large ships during the wars of the first half of the twentieth century forced shipbuilders to break with the slow conventional process of laying the keel, framing the hull, and outfitting the ship. They introduced prefabrication and grand block assembly to allow more simultaneous production that dramatically reduced completion times. (Images: The Mariners' Museum/Corbis, Kvaerner Philadelphia Shipyard Inc.)*

was concentrated almost entirely in the first stages of fabrication and interior fit-out and painting were relegated to the last stages. As more and more equipment and systems have been installed in contemporary ships, the fit-out of chambers within the hull has become increasingly complex. These chambers are often very confined spaces that can be accessed only through narrow passages and openings located a great distance from the upper decks of the ship. All materials, parts, and tools needed for the final stages of construction must be carried through labyrinthine passages, one by one, to their final installation destination in spaces that have little working room.

The construction process is no longer linear and it no longer proceeds solely from the bottom up.

Why are grand blocks a good idea? First, grand blocks have made an end-run around gravity. The construction process is no longer linear and it no longer proceeds solely from the bottom up. All trades can work from the outset on the various smaller segments of the ship. These segments are in simultaneous production, a process that yields a shorter overall construction duration. Grand blocks can even be built vertically for easy access and installation within compartments and then rotated into horizontal position for final installation at the dry dock.

Second, grand blocks can be built indoors where there are no weather stoppages and temperatures are relatively comfortable. Tools and equipment are nearby. Work space is less crowded. Inspections can be undertaken and problems corrected with each grand block while it is still in the controlled indoor work environment. The quality of construction improves.

Third, since grand blocks require less total work time to build than a comparable segment in a ship built entirely in dry dock, the cost of labor declines. The "1-3-8" rule of shipbuilding applies here: Any

SMART GRAND BLOCK

AND

SMART MODULE

ADDING INTELLIGENCE   *The integration of systems in the production of grand blocks has increased in sophistication over the years. Today, ships use "smart" modules that incorporate new technologies. For example, electric propulsion units are now simply plugged into the stern of a ship. These smart modules contain the entire motor housing and can operate independently of other systems. Now, if a problem with the motor occurs, a spare can simply be switched with the old, eliminating downtime. (Images: courtesy ABB Group, Hill Phoenix.)*

given task takes 1 hour in shop, 3 hours at site but off-hull, 8 hours inside hull. Less time, lower cost, higher quality. Grand blocks have obliterated linear assembly in shipbuilding.

Miniblocks are nested, like Russian dolls, within grand blocks. The shipbuilding industry has a double sense of the modularity concept. On the one hand, the grand block is an outer shell, a very large factory-built module unto itself. Nested within grand blocks, on the other hand, are other smaller modules. Like grand blocks, these miniblocks are also factory-built, but they are small enough that they can be built anywhere and shipped to the assembly site for final installation within grand blocks. Although both grand blocks and miniblocks are modules, they have different origins and purposes. Production quality, speed of assembly, and cost drive grand block assembly methods throughout the shipbuilding industry, both commercial and military.

In the military sector, however, one finds a further sense of modularity in a nested interchangeable system. These latter modules tend to be *smart elements*, such as power distribution and control packages, light distribution and control systems, workstations, cabins and other accommodations, weapons, electronics, mast, freshwater production equipment, and deck machinery. The genesis of smart elements is a desire for exchangeability. Unlike a ship itself that may have a useful life of 30 to 50 years, the service life of these smart elements may be as short as 5 to 10 years.

For the military, the joining concept in construction is interface, not integration.

Smart modules are intentionally not integrated into the architecture of grand blocks because integration suggests difficulty in removal. The intent instead is to facilitate removal and exchange. Hence, the relation between part and whole in an interfacing module is based on the difference in life cycles in construction and technology, between dumb and smart.

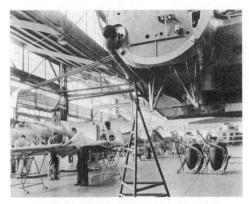

OLD: ACCUMULATION OF PIECES

AND

OLD: ASSEMBLY LINE

PRODUCTION EVOLUTION   *The aerospace industry has seen major shifts in its production paradigm over the course of the twentieth century. Initially, aircraft were a single-craft affair in which parts would be made, brought to one location, and assembled piece by piece. When the assembly line was introduced, roles were reversed, and the object would then move to where the parts were. (Images: Air Force Historical Research Agency, collections of Henry Ford Museum & Greenfield Village.)*

4.3   AIRPLANES

Boeing's wide-body plant in Everett, Washington, is no building we know. It is a manufacturing landscape so vast that it has become its own world. It has streets through it. It has scaffolding arrays so huge that they seem like scalable canyon or urban walls. We used to think Ledoux envisioned big rooms, but his vast interiors would be little more than cabins inside this enormous 95-acre, 11-story-high room. The structure of this room supports the world's largest roof, but it is first and foremost a scaffold for a network of cranes. These cranes slide overhead, beeping as they go, forever shifting along the *X, Y,* and *Z* axes of the landscape. In the dead of night, scaffolded steel-plate floors fold up, allowing the cranes to lift and transport large 777 modules from one work station to another. During the day, the cranes move smaller modules about from site to site.

The word *module* is used extensively in the aircraft industry. Parts, as we once knew them, no longer exist in this world. Instead, there are only collections of former parts conglomerated into a much smaller number of modules. Where are these modules made? For Boeing, the answer is "anywhere," depending upon politics, exchange rates, cost, and the engineering and manufacturing ability of the supplier. The Boeing 777 program has over 40 major suppliers who produce modules in more than a dozen countries. The aircraft skin panels are digitally described at Boeing then manufactured by Kawasaki Heavy Industries in Japan. For very large aircraft like the 777, the skins we see are panel modules, fragments of fuselage covers. For smaller aircraft such as the 737, the entire fuselage is made off site and shipped to the point of final assembly. Boeing describes this as part of a broadly based *monolithic design initiative*. Using the conventional definition of the word *part*, the 777's designers estimate there are more than one million.

The work of monolithic design initiatives is the same everywhere: to aggregate many parts into fewer modules before the point of final assembly. The purpose is to achieve higher quality, better features,

NEW: MODULAR PRODUCTION

JOINING MODULES   *The current method of aircraft production is based on modules that are fabricated in diverse locations and put together at the point of final assembly. The fuselage shown above is being lowered into the final assembly jig by means of a laser leveling system that ensures precise positioning. The entire assembly went together in just four weeks. (Images: Boeing.)*

less time to fabricate, and lower cost: more art and craft, not less. At Boeing, these efforts go even further as engineers seek ways to design and make into singular elements several parts that were once monolithic casts or machined entities. These are the ultimate modules; they are made of parts that never were, parts that have been recombined into modules.

An example of this initiative is the Boeing tail assembly. By changing the design to composite materials, the number of parts was reduced by nearly 800 for this one module alone, and the weight was reduced by 1,650 pounds, which increased the range by 78 miles. The substitution of materials is often the agent that transforms a process by eliminating some parts and enhancing the integration of the remaining parts.

Along the *X,Y,* and *Z* axes of the unending Boeing interior, neatly crated and unpacked modules awaiting final installation people the landscape of structure, cranes, and scaffolds. In the sequence of production, first comes the wing buildup. This module is largely made in the plant in a separate operation that includes joining the engine pylons to the wing. The second stage of production is concentrated on sections of the fuselage frame, already sheathed, beginning with the forward fuselage and working back to the central fuselage where the wings join the body. Landing gear and wing flaps are installed, and finally the rear cabin is aligned and leveled with the central fuselage by use of a laser. Each module of this stage arrives at the point of final assembly complete with much of its infrastructure, including Kevlar air ducts. In the third stage, the tail section is installed. In the fourth, the entire fuselage assembly is seal-tested then painted to resist corrosion, and in the fifth, the engines are installed. In the sixth stage, wiring harnesses and other infrastructural systems that extend between modules are installed. Here, electronic wiring is not done one strand at a time, but rather arrives at the point of final assembly spooled 50 together and fed through

VISIONARY ARCHITECTURE PROPOSED

VS.

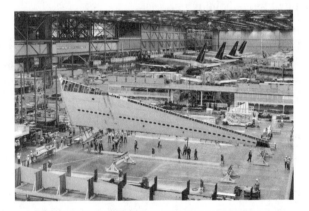

VISIONARY ARCHITECTURE REALIZED

PUSHING THE ENVELOPE *To create the successful automated world of the Boeing plant in Everett, WA, a building of a volume never seen before outside of the drawings of Boullée had to be created. The total volume of the plant is estimated at 472.4 million cubic feet. (Images: Leonard de Selva/Corbis, Boeing.)*

the fuselage in unison off the spool. In the seventh and final stage, the interior fit-out is completed. Many modules arrive fully assembled for installation, including bathrooms, kitchens, and closets.

The fabrication of certain modules may begin off site as much as 14 to 16 months in advance of delivery. This assembly tactic allowed even the earliest aircraft to be fabricated at the point of final assembly in 123 days. By 1997, the time had been cut to 38 days. With the reduction in time have come substantial savings in the cost of production.

SINGULAR CRAFT 1900

ASSEMBLY LINE 1920

VS.

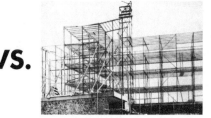

SINGULAR CRAFT 1900-2003

MODULARIZED 2003

CONTINUING INNOVATION   *The automobile industry, like the aerospace industry, has seen tremendous paradigm shifts in production throughout its history. The movement from single craft assembly at the turn of the century to assembly-line production two decades later, and now to modular production has, led, at each shift, to significant improvements in the quality and cost of automobiles. (Images: from the collections of Henry Ford Museum & Greenfield Village.)*

4.4   CARS

What does modular design mean to a process engineer? Cars, like most complex things, are made up of many parts, approximately 4,000, about 100 of which are key parts. The nineteenth-century cars were at first built one by one. Each was a singular craft affair, the way most buildings continue to be built today.

With the advent of mass production at Henry Ford's manufacturing and assembly plant in Detroit, most automobile production soon became a matter of gathering parts one by one for assembly along a moving line, with each worker installing the same part over and over on different vehicles as they passed stationary work stations. Gradually, car makers began to use outside manufacturers, not just as sources of parts but for fabrication of subassemblies. Process engineers began to realize the advantage of fragmenting cars, and developing them in *chunks*, or collections of parts. When these chunks were fabricated into components before arrival at the point of final assembly, gains could be made in quality and features while reductions were achieved in cost and time of fabrication.

The jarring difference between the new and old methods is amply evident in two Daimler-Chrysler plants in Toledo, Ohio, one of which produces Liberties and the other Jeeps. The Liberty plant is among those new plants designed to maximize the use of the techniques of modular assembly. The Jeep plant is its opposite. Here Jeeps are made in much the same way as they were built during World War II. The Liberty plant is itself a machine, a "clean-room" for the making of cars. Module and parts management is largely automated. Silent, unmanned delivery vehicles determine the required location of each part by means of a laser bounced off the building's structural grid and move both modules and parts to final assembly locations on demand. In a vast paint shop 100,000 square feet large, fully auto-mated, and remote controlled, 20 workers per shift paint 200 cars per day during two 10-hour shifts. There are few parts in sight, only enough for the work immediately at hand.

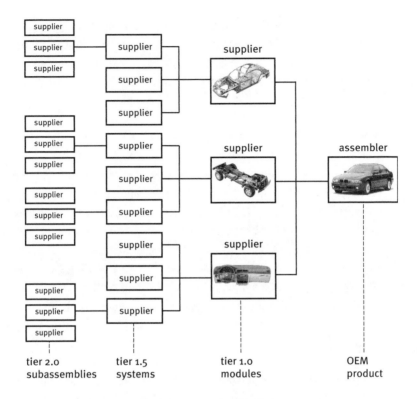

| tier 2.0 | tier 1.5 | tier 1.0 | OEM |
| subassemblies | systems | modules | product |

MODULAR PRODUCTION

THE MODULAR PRODUCTION SUPPLY CHAIN *The hierarchical tree for parts supply in the automobile industry is broken down into four levels, or tiers. It begins with an oem who subcontracts out the production of many large chunks of a vehicle. Those sub-contractors in turn sub out the smaller chunks of their modules. This ladder continues until a chunk is reduced to pure parts.*

As in a mass-production system, the assembly line moves, not the worker, but there have been elaborate transformations of the work platforms to accommodate the human body. Each task has been ergonomically engineered to reduce the stress on the worker's joints and muscles. The car moves up and down to accommodate the human body instead of having the body move to fit the car. Tools are immediately at hand. Tasks that require repeated heavy lifting are now accomplished by robots.

Car doors are painted along with the rest of the body to assure color match, then detached to allow ready access for work on the interior. The doors are fabricated as modules on an independent conveyor system that returns each door to the same body it came from at the end of assembly. The engine is inserted as a single unit, as are the cockpit, seats, rolling chassis, and front and rear quarters. Fewer parts, less time, higher quality, and enhanced features all are the results of assembly by module.

The production chain is condensed so that as few parts as possible arrive at the point of final assembly.

Both the process of design and the actual fabrication of cars have evolved swiftly before the accelerating wave of modular assembly. To accomplish this objective, the supplier chain is consolidated and hierarchically organized into tiers, modules, or chunks for arrival at the original equipment manufacturer (OEM), the company that bears the brand name.

The effects of preassembly on final production in the automotive industry have been dramatic. Underlying the results is the initially counterintuitive realization that quality is better controlled by fragmenting assembly. The more one attempts to undertake at the point of final assembly, the more difficult it is to control quality. Fewer joints in the final installation give rise to more precise tolerances and better working conditions with less accumulation of parts in the

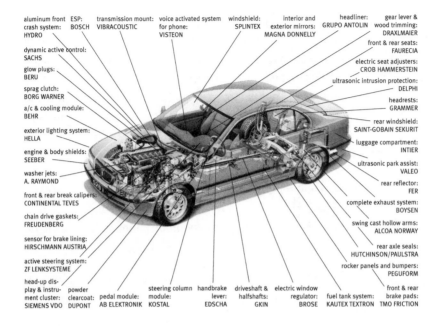

aluminum front crash system: HYDRO — ESP: BOSCH — transmission mount: VIBRACOUSTIC — voice activated system for phone: VISTEON — windshield: SPLINTEX — interior and exterior mirrors: MAGNA DONNELLY — headliner: GRUPO ANTOLIN — gear lever & wood trimming: DRAXLMAIER

dynamic active control: SACHS

glow plugs: BERU

sprag clutch: BORG WARNER

a/c & cooling module: BEHR

exterior lighting system: HELLA

engine & body shields: SEEBER

washer jets: A. RAYMOND

front & rear break calipers: CONTINENTAL TEVES

chain drive gaskets: FREUDENBERG

sensor for brake lining: HIRSCHMANN AUSTRIA

active steering system: ZF LENKSYSTEME

head-up display & instrument cluster: SIEMENS VDO — powder clearcoat: DUPONT — pedal module: AB ELEKTRONIK — steering column module: KOSTAL — handbrake lever: EDSCHA — driveshaft & halfshafts: GKIN — electric window regulator: BROSE — fuel tank system: KAUTEX TEXTRON — front & rear brake pads: TMO FRICTION

front & rear seats: FAURECIA

electric seat adjusters: CROB HAMMERSTEIN

ultrasonic intrusion protection: DELPHI

headrests: GRAMMER

rear windshield: SAINT-GOBAIN SEKURIT

luggage compartment: INTIER

ultrasonic park assist: VALEO

rear reflector: FER

complete exhaust system: BOYSEN

swing cast hollow arms: ALCOA NORWAY

rear axle seals: HUTCHINSON/PAULSTRA

rocker panels and bumpers: PEGUFORM

A FINE QUILT

A HARMONIOUS SUPPLY CHAIN   *Some of today's finest cars that we associate with major brands are in fact made up almost entirely of parts manufactured by other companies. The best car manufacturers have become the best managers of their supply chains. (Image: courtesy BMW AG.)*

final assembly area. Further, when responsibility for the car is fragmented into modules, there are more entities assuming primary responsibility for their quality than in the earlier command-and-control method of construction. The overall result is that the suppliers in aggregate direct more resources on the design and making of components than the OEM did when all fabrication was centralized under the sole agency of the brand-name manufacturer.

Over the past several years, modular assembly has permeated the techniques of nearly all car manufacturers.

Modular assemblies can be made by any number of suppliers in three types of location: in facilities located anywhere in the world that offer shipment to the point of final assembly, in supplier parks adjacent to or near final assembly plants, or in facilities operated by the suppliers but attached to the final assembly plants.

Increasingly, OEMS are demanding that suppliers attach facilities to their assembly plants to maximize flexibility and to minimize both shipping time and the expense of handling materials. The resulting architectural type is one of feeders, above-grade roots that supply the factory with predigested parts. These suppliers are expressed in terms of tiers. For instance, a Tier 2 supplier is far downstream from the assembly plant and might produce only screws and fasteners, a Tier 1.5 supplier might manufacture radios, whereas a Tier 1 supplier is responsible for the complete dashboard. The number of Tier 1 *mega-suppliers* increased more than threefold between 1992 and 2000. Many smaller Tier 2 and Tier 1.5 parts suppliers have been consolidated with Tier 1 suppliers to provide modular assemblies to OEMS. For those willing and able to become integrators, many opportunities have opened to move up in the food chain and become more than a parts supplier. Production has gained in efficiency with the increase in modular assembly by outside suppliers. As a result of recent productivity gains in the last seven years, cost reductions have been enjoyed in three categories: production labor (33.7 percent), design (33.7 percent), and materials (16.4 percent).

LESS IS MORE

LESS IS A BORE

MORE FOR LESS

MODERNITY PROGRESSES ONCE AGAIN *Architecture of the twentieth century initially taught us that simplicity and purity was the way to achieve a richness in meaning. This ultimately gave way to complexity and contradiction as an attempt to achieve the same thing. The twenty-first century, however, has combined both precedents and aims at generating even more content while spending and using less. It is a principle of lean economy. (Images: Artifice Inc., Johnson Controls.)*

The average overall savings in the manufacturing cost of a car in 1999 were 14.9 percent when compared to manufacturing in 1996. While the results were surprising and dramatic in the aggregate, some of the individual findings were even more unexpected. Savings in the cost of materials were derived from modular designs that use less materials with less waste to attain better quality results-more for less. Examples of modular chunks include door systems, seating systems, the rolling chassis and engine exterior, front and rear corners, and cockpit systems.

If you do not believe that less is more, anyone can get you more for more, but it takes genius to get more for less.

A car cockpit that is built using traditional methods of assembly has 104 parts that weigh 138 pounds and take 22.4 minutes to install. Using modular assembly, the 104 parts are reduced to one and the installation time decreases to 3.3 minutes. Even the total mass decreases to 123 pounds as a result of modular preassembly. The total savings in labor and materials per cockpit in 1999 dollars is $79. One of the parts that makes up the cockpit is the steel structure required as a scaffold to support the myriad parts of the cockpit, the heaviest of which is the ventilation, heating, and cooling system for the car interior. In addition to its function as armature, this beam contributes to the cabin's resistance to impact in the event of a crash. By combining and integrating previously separate functions, could the structural beam also be a duct for the heating, cooling, and ventilating system? Could structure and air distribution be accomplished by the same part, and could a weight reduction be effected at the same time? If fiber-reinforced resins were formed into a hollow beam with air outlets, could the resulting single, lighter part be made as strong or stronger than its steel predecessor? Yes. Would quality be enhanced? Yes, owing to the presence of far fewer joints and the elimination of separate ducts and structure.

THE ART OF JOINERY

THE FETISH OF THE JOINT *In construction, architects are happy to receive half-inch tolerances. In the car industry, precision is measured in millimeters. (Image: Tom Nagy/photographer and Johnny Wujek and Maya Rubin/models 2001.)*

4.5   THE ARCHITECTURE OF THE JOINT

This new architecture requires different theories and forms of join-ing. The joint used to be a part-by-part certainty. If you had a part, there would be at least one, or even many, joints between it and other parts. When assemblages, be they cars, ships, aircraft, or buildings, were constructed one part at a time, from the bottom up, then from the frame inward and outward, the art of joining was a craft that developed to resolve the relations among a vast number of parts. In this past world, joints arose principally from physical prop-erties and limitations of size in materials. Since thermal expansion and contraction of materials generates movement, a central purpose of the joint has been the management of movement. Joints also sep-arated dissimilar materials and permitted the joining of similar materials that individually could not be fabricated or transported in the size required by their proposed use.

Nearly all complex artifacts are made up of many parts that require joints. The objective of modular joining is not necessarily to limit the total number of joints that are present in a given artifact. Instead, the focus is on geography, on the location of the plant where the materials are actually joined. The least desirable place to join mate-rials is the point of final assembly, at the far end of the material sup-ply chain. Joining theory was once hierarchical, with most materials being joined at the place of final assembly: a car at the OEM assem-bly plant, a ship in a dry dock, a plane in an assembly hanger. The theory was that a command-and-control structure would assure quality and manage cost by keeping as much work under the final assembler's direct control as possible. In a contemporary theory and practice that recognizes the essentially chaotic nature of assem-bling complex artifacts, the focus is instead on disassembling the process into smaller integrated component assemblies. These smaller chunks can then be designed and managed in their own right, as completed artifacts, by a separate team focused solely on a piece of the overall product. Quality control can be managed incre-mentally, one module at a time, with corrections made before final assembly. Further, there is less product to clutter work spaces,

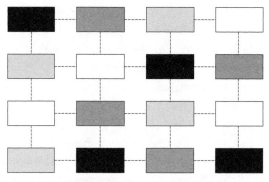

24 JOINTS AT FINAL ASSEMBLY

VS.

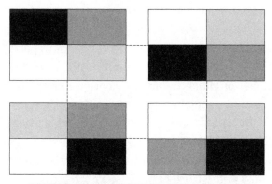

4 JOINTS WITH COMPONENT ASSEMBLY

REDUCTION THEORY   *The concept behind using component assemblies to reduce the number of joints at final assembly is simple: prejoin elements. If joints can be broken down into smaller groups and those groups can then be joined, the number of final joints is reduced.*

enhanced efficiency and safety, and less chance to install the wrong component during final assembly.

The mathematics underlying this theory of joining is powerful. Simply stated, the relation between the number of parts in an artifact and the potential interfaces between those parts is exponential: Two parts have one interface (2:1); 4 parts have 4 possible interfaces (1:1) and 16 parts generate 24 potential interfaces among those parts (2:3). The average car has 4,000 parts. Each of these interfaces between two of its parts is a joint with—in equal measure—an opportunity for either craft or crisis.

When we make any artifact, we tend to focus on pieces, on the parts and their features. An automotive supply catalog is a list of parts. There is no comparable catalog of automotive joints, yet potential joints outnumber parts by an ever-increasing exponential ratio. The amount of energy required during design and fabrication to resolve all the joining problems in the design and making of any artifact is staggering. First, each joint is itself a problem. The engineer or designer defines the problem. The objectives for the solution and the constraints that must be satisfied by the joint are identified. Each joint then requires an act of design either by selection or by custom-design. Each of these potential interfaces between parts must be developed. Engineers and designers respond to this complexity by developing functional typologies for joints. Still, the number of modifications of types required is considerable.

Now take the mathematics of joining onto the assembly floor or to the building site. Each joint is now a matter of craft. Each of the million or so possible permutations in a Boeing 777 must be accurately assembled and crafted within a fixed time constraint. The sheer volume of parts at the point of final assembly is a logistical log jam. Shortcomings in quality in this method of assembly were inevitable, as were issues of productivity and cost.

TIER 2 JOINTS = 100+

TIER 1.5 JOINTS = 10+

TIER 1 JOINTS = 1+

PUTTING THEORY TO PRACTICE *The seat module shown above illustrates how the joint reduction theory works in the automobile industry. The effectiveness of component assembly increases as more systems and joints are included in the modules. (Images: courtesy Delphi Corporation, DaimlerChrysler.)*

The solution was found in the mathematics of joining. If more parts generate exponentially more joints, then the opposite is also true: fewer parts generate exponentially fewer joints. There are two possible solutions: fragment the assembly process and reduce the number of parts. A reduction in parts requires a complete redesign of the parts themselves and often the materials used to make them. It is more difficult and takes more time to research and test redesigned parts than it does to redesign the process. Since time is an expensive commodity, most manufactures have focused first on fragmenting the design and assembly process into discrete pieces: modules, chunks, grand blocks. These modules, chunks, or grand blocks are composed of a similar array of pieces as was previously the case: they are simply fabricated at some distance from the point of final assembly. The problem of joining does not go away but shifts to another location. The changed locus, however, is a significant part of the solution. A very complex problem is made into a series of smaller, less complex ones. Design resolution can be more focused, and there is less complexity to deal with in the final assembly process. A new central design problem arises however, in how to join at the scale of modules, chunks, and grand blocks.

Although joints must still resolve the limitations in the physical properties of materials in this world of modular design, joints are no longer simply a solution to that single problem. They are now as much, or more, a question of the hierarchy in the supply chain. Joints now, in fact, parallel the supply chain. We used to have dovetail and butt joints. We now have the following types of joint: Tier 1.5 supplier joints; Tier 1 supplier joint; Assembler (OEM) joints.

Tier 1.5 joints are similar to the joints of yesterday. They are produced by a supplier who gathers a modest number of parts and joins them into a new system, such as the heating, ventilating, and air conditioning system for a car or a radio. The presence of a joint at this level signifies any or all of several possibilities that derive from classical joining theory. There may be a change in the materials best suited to accommodate the function; there may be an alteration in

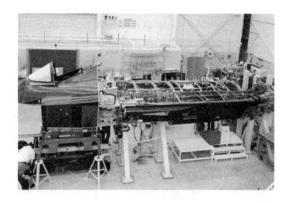

SELF-JIGGING JOINTS

JOINT INDEPENDENCE *The key to creating chunks or modules is that they must be able to exist as completed entities that can support themselves without any armature until the point of final assembly. (Image: Boeing.)*

required geometry that cannot be accomplished by a single part; there may be properties of material that limit size in a way that is insufficient to function.

Tier 1 joints, however, are a new breed. For example, the assemblage of 104 individual parts into an auto cockpit in a Delphi Systems factory is a new method for joining complex parts in off-site factories. These 104 parts do not arrive for fabrication at the point of final assembly but rather at a 180,000-square-foot factory located about 3.5 miles away from the customer, in this case a car assembly plant in Lansing, Michigan, that belongs to General Motors, the maker of the Grand Am and Malibu. A signal from the paint shop in this car assembly plant triggers the fabrication of the cockpit module at the Delphi plant across town. There are approximately 1,000 different possible configurations for these cockpit modules. Remarkably, the maximum total time from the broadcast signal to build a custom cockpit to its delivery at the assembly plant is 105 minutes.

What is different about Tier 1 joints? The cockpit chunk or module must be conceived to stand on its own as a completed structure. It cannot require any armature or support beyond itself during fabrication, shipping, and installation. Once the *build document*, a specification sheet describing the particular product to be built, arrives electronically with the signal to build, the appropriate steel tubular frame—the armature for the entire module—is placed upon a conveyor that rotates the frame into ergonomically appropriate positions for each successive task. An astonishingly lightweight heating, ventilating, and air conditioning system is fastened to the frame, along with complex, prepackaged wiring harnesses that interconnect dozens of electronic functions. *Pick-time*, the time required to get the part to the module, is reduced through the use of custom preformed racks at the assembly line. A plastic duct is fastened between the frame and the air handler. *Cluster-sequencing* ensures that parts arrive at the line in the correct order of assembly, so that

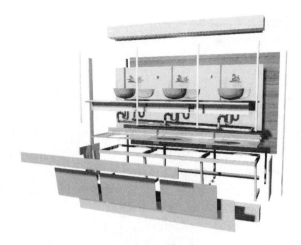

200 JOINTS ON SITE

NECESSARY EVIL   *Anything that has many parts will have many associated joints. Joining elements on site is inefficient and often sloppily executed. The vanity assembly above has approximately 200 joints of various types.*

VS.

1 JOINT ON SITE

THE FINAL ASSEMBLY JOINT   *The ultimate goal of the component assembly process and joint reduction is to leave just one joint type at the moment of final assembly or installation. What was formerly 200 joints in the field has now become essentially one at the site to install the assembly. The fabrication occurs in a factory, where a controlled environment makes the process of joining more efficient with higher precision.*

no selection by the installer is necessary. Every 15 seconds, two shifts a day, a mass-customized completed cockpit module leaves the line.

The Tier 1 joints embedded within this module differ from Tier 1.5 joints in that they are not holistically integrated into the total artifact, whether car, ship, or aircraft. Instead, Tier 1 joints are designed to form a stand-alone module, a subassembly of parts that can be fabricated physically independently of the total artifact. These parts depend upon and are joined in successive layers to each other and ultimately to a subframe.

Embedded within the module, however, is yet another breed of joint: final assembly joints. These are the joints that provide the means of connection, systems interface, and closure between the modules and systems that comprise a complex artifact such as a car, ship, or aircraft. Connection joints fasten one module to another physically. They are the means by which the independently fabricated cockpit is joined to the overall armature of the car. Systems connections are joints that allow systems to be fabricated in modules or chunks, independent of the frame, then joined to other systems in other modules at the final assembly plant. These joints are typically a new form of quick-coupled connections. If the system is electrical, a plug connection provides the interface instead of a hardwired connection or a junction box. If the system is hydronic, a quick-coupling joins the tubing. If it is an air system, such as a duct, a slip-sleeve may provide the joint. Lastly, closure joints provide the visual finish of the module as its surfaces are closed to other modules. These joints that we see come in many forms. Typically today we do not see the actual connector, which lies hidden below. Instead, the visual representation of the joint may be a reveal, or a controlled gap, between materials or a lap-joint where one part slides within another. The visual relation between the parts may in turn be flush, subflush, or projecting. The assembly processes for all these joints ensure quality control through built-in registers that render it impossible for parts to be misaligned. They simply will not fit together at all if they are not aligned properly.

V

ARCHITECTURE

LE CORBUSIER 1910

BUCKMINSTER FULLER 1930

FRANK LLOYD WRIGHT 1940

WALTER GROPIUS 1960

OPERATION BREAKTHTOUGH 1970

A CENTURY OF FAILURES *The modernists of the twentieth century made many attempts to adopt mass production, prefabrication and modularization techniques in their buildings. None of these endeavors ever achieved success or popularity and soon were abandoned. (Images: (first)2003 Artists Rights Society New York/ADAGP Paris/FLC, (second) Wichita-Sedgwick County Historical Museum, (fourth) Busch-Reisinger Museum, Harvard University Art Museums, (fifth) U.S. Department of Housing and Urban Development.)*

5.1   A CENTURY OF FAILURE

A fervent desire to convert modern architecture into a commodity, to turn away from permanence and toward transience, away from elitist and toward universal, pervades modern architectural theory. Although the dream has risen anew with each generation since the beginning of the twentieth century, it has failed to materialize with each successive incarnation. Italian Futurist Antonio St. Elia's vision of architectural implosion in which each generation must destroy its built inheritance then make anew and inhabit its own architecture, Le Corbusier's mass-produced housing modeled on American automotive production, numerous factory-produced houses of the World War II era, and the industrialized building program of Operation Breakthrough in the Nixon era all failed to provide lasting legacies.

The overarching reason for these failures was the restrictive nature of the agendas that underlay each successive effort.

Focus is normally a prerequisite for success. Here it has been fatal. It set the stage for the failure of each new vision. Each attempt to transform architecture into a commodity had political, programmatic, procedural, and stylistic agendas that were narrowly defined. Each fervent belief system was narrowly monotheistic and so had little widespread, enduring, self-sustaining applicability.

Twentieth-century dreams of an attainable off-site architecture were underpinned and motivated by political agendas that ranged in ideology from Marxist to liberal to social democratic. The difficulty in associating architectural production with Western politics lies in the cyclical nature of politics. While national and local political postures in many Western democracies can, and often are, altered every few years, architectural production does not thrive on rapid change. The production and support structures required to build are slow to evolve and expensive to implement. When these structures are tied to politics, they lack the continuity of capital expenditure and procedures required to sustain an enduring architectural agenda. In the United States and in other Western democracies, the market, not the government, is the only reliable long-term agent of change.

THE MASS PRODUCTION VISION

VS.

MASS PRODUCTION TODAY

LACK OF FRUITION *Le Corbusier's vision of adopting mass-production techniques to provide the working class with an improved "machine for living" never developed into what he had hoped for. Rather than elevate the standard for the working class, architecture elected to make banal, non-descript, shoe boxes that do not take advantage of the automated techniques to make a higher-quality product. (Image: 2003 Artists Rights Society New York/ADAGP Paris/FLC.)*

The other face of these political ideologies has been a programmatic focus on housing. By equating a process of building with a single type of building—housing—the result has again been disastrous to the modernist dream of an attainable industrialized architecture. Housing is only one portion of architectural production. By focusing on housing as the only type of building subject to off-site fabrication, the far more powerful idea of a generally applicable process has been lost. The potential of the off-site process is greatest when the breadth of its applicability is broadest. The focus on housing has stigmatized both the process of off-site fabrication and housing as a building type. Each is seen as less because of this unfortunate pairing.

In quality, off-site fabrication has come to be associated with products in trailer parks.

Mass production is a way to make a building that produces less for less. The opportunity to make an Architecture with a capital *A*, that is more for less has been squandered again and again.

One lesson that engineers understand and teach, but architects neglect, is that process sets the stage for outcome. Without a broadly based process that penetrates deeply into the very heart of how things are made, any success will be fleeting and unsustainable. Owing in large measure to the arrogance of its visionary architects, the past century has seen the failure of vision after vision of a new and better world of a more accessible architecture. Needed here to sustain the dream of an accessible architecture is a commitment to a pluralist process. Rather than the imposition of architectural vision on contemporary modes of construction, the process must be a broadly based fusion of all possibilities and capacities across the entire spectrum of those who make architecture. We need a new vision of process, not just product. Along with architects, the vision must include those who own and use architecture, those who

THE WHOLE WAS NOT GREATER THAN ITS PARTS

USING PROGRESSIVE METHODS TO ACHIEVE CONVENTIONAL RESULTS *One of the great failures of modularization attempts of the twentieth century was lack of variability. These elaborate kits of parts were unable to do more than assemble the one intended result. They did not improve upon existing paradigms. (Images: Arnold Newman/Getty Images, Ohio Historical Society.)*

assemble buildings, and those who develop materials and engineer the new products that become our architecture. The vision of an integrated process, in which a collective intelligence replaces the architect's singular imposed intelligence, must become widespread before off-site fabrication can become the standard means of architectural construction.

Lastly, there is the question of outward form, of appearance or, to use that much avoided term, style.

Nearly all efforts of twentieth-century architects to commodify architecture have been accompanied by an idiosyncratic agenda about appearance.

Early in the twentieth century, the appearance of the new architecture was a direct outcome of the reductive nature of the new assembly methods. Le Corbusier, for instance, posited a pure form for each type of production as the lowest common denominator of design and fabrication. His industrialized "object types" became the style and the substance of the new architecture of his time. Le Corbusier acknowledged that the "right state of mind" did not then exist for his new, iterative, mass-produced architecture but predicted it would only be 20 years for this transformation in rational methods of construction to come to pass. He was right. It did come to pass, but the spirit of living in mass-production houses did not. Individual circumstances of cultural heritage, personal preference, and particulars of site, while not consistent, are always present and will always work against any impulse toward a common, repetitive appearance and substance for all production. Furthermore, repetitive appearance and substance are no longer a prerequisite for off-site fabrication. By decoupling appearance from substance and emphasizing the substance of new methods of fabrication we can exploit the multiplicity of form they give rise to. We also eliminate a persistent reason that transformative off-site assembly failed to take hold.

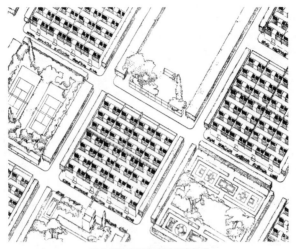

MASS PRODUCTION

VS.

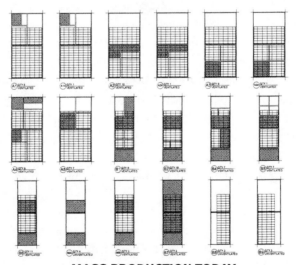

MASS PRODUCTION TODAY

INCORPORATING FLEXIBILITY   *The difference today that will enable modularization and mass production to succeed is its ability to be customizable. No longer does mass production have to produce the same repeated product; now flexible production methods allow for customization on a large scale. (Image: 2003 Artists Rights Society New York/ADAGP Paris/FLC.)*

5.2 THE CENTURY OF THE REALIZABLE DREAM

Why can we succeed now, given a century-long legacy of failure and disappointment? What has changed today? In a word: Everything. Nothing is the same.

Mass customization is rapidly replacing mass production. Mass production was all about the economy of making things in quantity, but mass customization does not depend on quantity to be cost effective. Mass customization is about cultural production as opposed to the industrial output of mass production. In other words, rather than decide among options produced by industry, the customer determines what the options will be by participating in the flow of the design process from the very start.

Furthermore, our clients are insisting on change. It is no longer acceptable to report year in and year out that architecture costs more, takes longer to build, and yields lower quality. We risk irrelevance if we continue to refuse change. By contrast, we invite a return to our former privileged position as master builders when we become the agents of change.

The single, most important change from Le Corbusier's vision has been the shift in fabrication from mass production to mass customization.

For nearly all of the twentieth century, the theoretical and practical basis of the efforts to realize off-site fabrication was sameness. The Model T was a compelling image for architects because of its unrelenting adherence to replication. Le Corbusier felt the power of this idea and promoted its adoption by architecture. Not only would the physical world become more beautiful and powerful through its reduction to "object types," he believed, but these "object types" would both cost less and broaden society's access to well-designed commodities of high quality, whether they were cars or buildings.

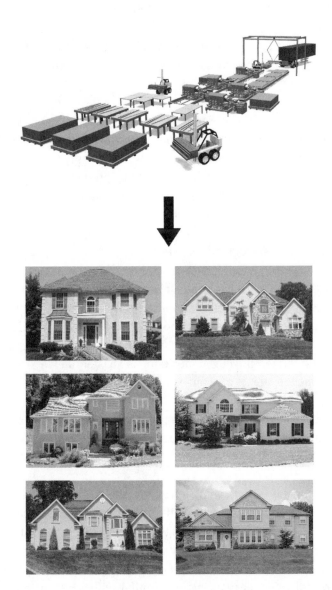

AUTOMATING MEDIOCRITY

THE BOTTOM LINE   *The unfortunate reality of the current usage of automated production techniques in building is that it is only serving the most mediocre of projects. There is no reason why all levels of architecture should not take advantage of the processes that enable us to build faster, cheaper, and with the potential for higher levels of quality.*

The fundamental problem with mass production for architecture was then, and remains now, its lack of mass appeal. The only substantial market for mass-produced architecture fabricated off site developed under the economic, material, and labor constraints of World War II. There was little mass appeal in 1920 for mass-produced architecture, and there remains little mass appeal for this idea today.

Where there is sameness, time will differentiate. For the twenty-first century, however, we no longer have to wait for time; we have within our reach methods of mass fabrication that yield custom results. Just as the cpu of a computer can be customized over the telephone, along with hundreds of other formerly mass-produced products, so too can architecture be mass customized to fit the specific circumstances of site and owner's preference. Modular construction is no longer a slave to mass production, repetition, and sameness. Even the word "modular" has itself been replaced by "off site." Eighty to ninety percent of the work required to build many custom structures can now be performed in a factory off site; slavish repetition of a product is no longer necessary to render this method of production viable.

Not only did Le Corbusier's "necessary state of mind" not exist but, even more importantly, the very discipline of off-site construction had yet to be invented.

Factories, custom machinery and equipment, lifting devices, and transportation systems all had to be created and developed before a market for off-site construction could come into being. Building codes had to be developed and modified, and local code officials had to be educated. Labor forces had to be recruited and trained to think about and fabricate buildings that begin their life by moving, by defying rather than submitting to gravity. All these old obstacles to mass production have been breached. The vernacular off-site industry already has the capacity to build off site in nearly all materials, including steel, concrete, and masonry. The only thing lacking is the vision and the will to use it.

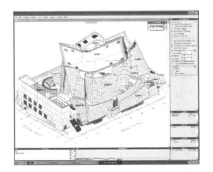

ARCHITECTURE & BUILDING

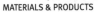

MATERIALS & PRODUCTS

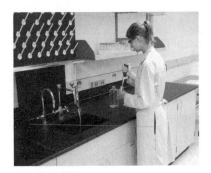

A BUILT EXAMPLE

THE COLLECTIVE INTELLIGENCE OF THE WALT DISNEY CONCERT HALL BY GEHRY AND ASSOCIATES
The Los Angeles concert hall typifies the type of collective intelligence architecture rarely sees. A wealth of shared knowledge had to be orchestrated by the architects in order to accomplish a project that required such a high level of sophistication and coordination. (Images: (concert hall photos) Federico Zignani/artdrive.org.)

5.3   PURE CREATION OF COLLECTIVE INTELLIGENCE

Not only can we now change the construction paradigm from mass production to mass customization, but now we must. The world, and our clients, have seen what has been accomplished in other manufacturing fields: ships, airplanes, and cars. Higher quality and added scope and features are there, along with lower cost and shorter time to fabricate. The old equilibrium between cost and time no longer holds. The mandate for change has now shifted to architecture. We cannot continue to build architecture at ever higher costs, longer schedules, and lower quality. We must act. We can return to master building. We can reestablish craft in architecture by integrating the intelligence of the architect, contractor, materials scientist, and product engineer into a collective web of information.

Architecture built in a factory in sections that come together for the first time in the field requires new ways to control, manage, and distribute information about design and construction.

In a building conventionally erected in the field, the building itself is conceived and built whole. The conventional construction of architecture is a process that provides continual feedback to designers and builders about the continuity and fit of various elements at each sequential stage of assembly in the field. The architect today begins by representing an idea of the desired outcome. Later, fabrication drawings detail the methods of assembly to be used to effect the desired outcome. Nonetheless, the knowledge about fit and connection is incomplete at conception. Trial and error in the field is used throughout the conventional building process. The building is both prototype and completed architecture. When parts do not fit, the mismatched construction is either removed and rebuilt, or else different parts are substituted.

The conventional method of field-fitting adjacent pieces, element by element, will not work with integrated components that are assembled off-site. In off site construction, the components must fit, since

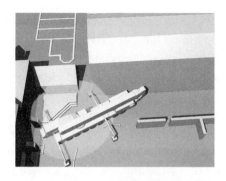

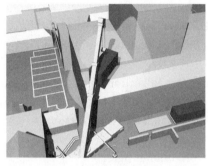

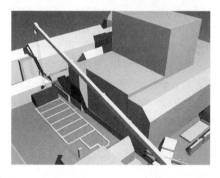

TROUBLESHOOTING AT THE DESIGN STAGE

DETERMINING THE TROUBLE SPOTS IN CRANING MODULAR ELEMENTS ONTO A POTENTIAL SITE
Solid modeling and virtual mock-ups provide architects with the advantage of foreseeing many potential problems. Logistics can be worked out in a virtual environment to strategize accurately for the field.

they arrive at the site whole and, in most cases, cannot readily be modified. In fact, field modifications erode the advantages of off-site fabrication.

Fortunately, today's information-control systems can manage off-site fabrication through intranets and extranets and multidimensional simulations. We can now solid-model components and simulate how they will join all adjacent elements. Instead of field testing, we can even virtual test certain components and assemblies to predict the performance of their structures and systems. There are programs that allow us to understand quantities, cost, and time of assembly while we are designing. Bills of materials to be purchased, along with projections of cost and schedule, can be seamlessly integrated with design. Intranets and extranets allow us to communicate rapidly and regularly with affiliated designers. When the integrated component assemblies fabricated off site come together to form a complete building—architecture—at a remote site, we can now know exactly how the interfaces between the elements will join. We now have the tools to make this cooperation happen. The resolve to use them must rise to the same level of sophistication.

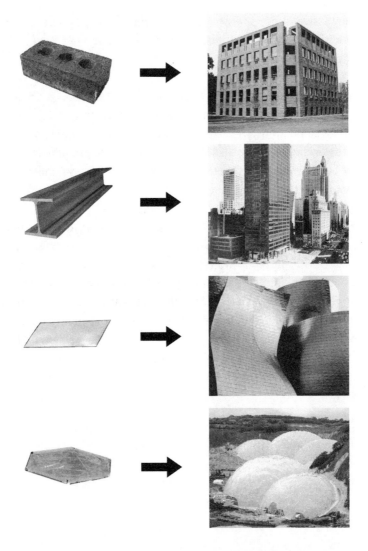

ASSOCIATIONS OF MATERIAL AND FORM

FORM FOLLOWS MATERIAL *Many twentieth-century modernist masters have contributed to establishing certain relationships between form and material. Their iconic works are recalled at the site of the materials which were used to create them. (Images: (Seagram Building) Bettmann/Corbis, (Guggenheim) Bilbao Zinat Yusufzai, (Eden Project) Graham Tim/Corbis SYGMA.)*

5.4   MATERIALITY INTO ARCHITECTURE

Form is the responsibility of the designer and the maker. The architecture of the first three-quarters of the past century, however, reminds us that new materials may indeed suggest new methods of assembly and give rise to new forms. The architecture of the last quarter of the century reestablished the understanding that there is no necessary, irrevocable relation between material and form.

The impact of new materials and processes on a building at the turn of the twentieth century has been well chronicled by Siegfried Gideon and others. The introduction of steel and the elevator allowed the tall building to develop, since heavy masonry was no longer required to transfer loads to the ground and the number of stories in a building was no longer limited by the number of flights a person could reasonably be expected to climb. Compared with the new steel, heavy masonry walls were counterproductive and uneconomic, and the practical agency of the elevator offered a new alternative to the stair or ramp, which before then were the only vertical transportation systems available. Similarly, Gideon famously described ways in which the balloon frame—a new method of assembly, not a new material—transformed residential architecture in the United States.

Material can be a progenitor of form.

The rate at which new materials have been introduced into architecture, viewed down its long history, has been very slow, nonexistent even for protracted periods of time. Stone, clay, masonry, wood, and thatch came first. Many centuries later, concrete was invented. Still later, metals were added, first as reinforcements and fasteners. Glass came into use as a building material about a thousand years ago, and the use of iron as a structural element is a nineteenth-century phenomenon. The rate at which new materials were invented and applied to architecture escalated dramatically during the twentieth century, especially after World War II. Even that dramatic

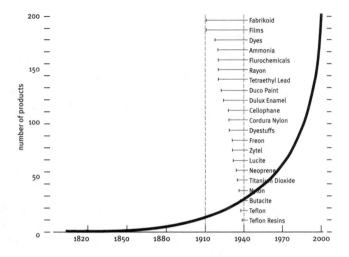

EXPLOSION OF NEW MATERIALS

NUMBER OF DUPONT PRODUCTS AVAILABLE THROUGHOUT HISTORY   *The rapid development of materials and products over the last 150 years has been exponential. Unfortunately, their incorporation into architecture has been relatively slow.*

increase, however, pales in comparison to the exponential explosion of new materials in the last quarter of the century.

We have only begun to speculate upon the uses of these new materials in architecture. Characteristic properties have begun to emerge however, in recently developed materials that are the opposite of many conventional materials now in widespread use. In general, conventional materials have a relatively low ratio of strength to density. A great deal of material is required to yield relatively little strength. The structural properties of the majority of recently invented materials invert this relationship. Relatively little material yields significantly greater strength than do comparable quantities of traditional materials.

Dramatic changes in the properties of recently developed materials will ultimately transform architecture yet again. The fascination with these thousands of new materials is evident everywhere. Material Connexion, a materials library, collects, catalogs, and displays thousands of new materials ranging from Aerogel to Zenite. The attraction of today's architects to new materials borders on infatuation. Novelty is often sufficient to justify use. Beyond infatuation, however, lies a world of purposeful form yet to be explored, a world in which materials will be selected based upon properties relevant to use.

VS.

IMPROVING WORKING CONDITIONS

MAKING WORK SAFER AND MORE COMFORTABLE   *As the automobile industry and shipbuilding industry have shown, moving work inside improves the working environment and increases opportunities for a larger worker pool. Advantages for workers such as ergonomic workbenches can be installed on a factory floor, an improvement over the jobsite. (Image: Lewis Hine/courtesy George Eastman House.)*

5.5   UNIONS

Labor skilled in field construction is becoming an increasingly rare commodity throughout the developed world. Labor shortages in some building trades are chronic, even in times of recession. Reports abound of desirable projects put out to bid finding no bids for a trade as simple as drywall installation and finishing. Fewer and fewer young people are choosing to enter into training programs for the trade. Why? The reasons are varied and include problems related to working conditions and safety. The environmental conditions that confront workers outdoors can be severe: too hot, too cold, too windy, too wet, too much snow or ice. All these discomforts can make work unpleasant, slow, and dangerous. At times weather conditions even make it impossible to work, requiring expensive overtime work to make up for lost time.

All these problems can be avoided by building the building inside a building.

By building the building inside a building, working conditions other than weather can also be improved. The relation between the tradesman's body and the work can be manipulated for greater comfort, less strain, and lower risk of the chronic injuries that can result from repetitive motions or work performed in awkward spaces. Indoors, safety can be enhanced by reducing aerial work and the use of ladders. In conventional construction, the worker goes to the task, moving from location to location, and carries all the materials and tools necessary. Productivity and safety can both be improved by bringing the task to the worker. Indoors, the tradesman has a fixed place to work that is outfitted with a full array of tools close to the task to be performed. We can improve working conditions for the construction trades and attract new workers, including women. We just have to build inside a building.

There is an unfounded fear that off-site fabrication will be seen as an encroachment on labor unions. There is no inherent threat to unions

PLUMBER

ELECTRICIAN

DRYWALLER

MASON   CARPENTER

CONSOLIDATING THE INDUSTRY

INCREASING COOPERATION AND PRODUCTIVITY *Many diverse groups represent the interests of the various building trades. They must constantly compete with each other for scheduling, money, and representation, which ultimately discourages cooperation and collaboration. Perhaps an umbrella organization that serves as a common forum for the diverse trades could solve this problem.*

in shifting the location of much of the labor that goes into making a building from outside to inside.

Union labor can be used just as readily when architecture is built inside the building as when it is built outside.

In fact, for all of the reasons cited above, a central objective of labor unions to improve working conditions can be realized most fully when the building is built under controlled interior conditions. For guidance we need only to look again at the example of the automotive industry. While cars have always been built inside buildings, much of their fabrication into large assemblages, or chunks, has shifted from the point of final assembly to adjacent and remote off-site assembly plants. Initially feared by labor unions, this shift was negotiated seamlessly by unions and manufacturers during the decade of the 1990s. The labor strife that characterized earlier decades has been largely eliminated through a new model for labor relations that focuses on improved working conditions, job security, and the participation of unions and workers in the organization and responsibility for work. As many building construction tasks shift from outside to inside, new umbrella unions can come into being that organize the multiplicity of trade unions under a single larger structure not unlike the United Auto Workers union. The current competition among unions in the construction trades can be replaced by a unified construction industry in which its workers are coordinated in a single, powerful, flexible entity capable of dissolving the arbitrary boundaries that limit productivity and quality.

1931 FORD

OR

1931 EMPIRE STATE BUILDING

MACHINE AND BUILDING WERE NOT EQUAL   *At the time of Vers une Architecture's publication, there was a great disparity between the automobile and the building. Automobiles incorporated many systems that drove the car as well as provided climate comfort for the driver. The building, on the other hand, was quite primitive and included a bare minimum of systems that had progressed only little from the turn of the century. (Images: Underwood & Underwood/Corbis; Photography Collection, Miriam D. Wallach Division of Art Prints and Photographs, New York Public Library, Astor Lenox and Tilden Foundations.)*

5.6   INCREASING COMPLEXITY

The theory of mass-produced architecture quickly became part of modern orthodoxy at the turn of the last century. The infatuation remained largely theoretical however, since there were many design demonstrations but no broadly based success. Yet a further reason for the failure of off-site fabrication to take deep root in the construction economy early in the twentieth century is the fact that building was still a simple affair—mostly structure and shelter with few systems—closer in spirit to Laugier's primitive hut than to the automobile it sought to imitate. Two measures of its simplicity are the number and cost of the systems in a turn-of-the-century building. In 1900, even a large building for a well-endowed institution might have only two systems: fireplaces for heat and light; and gutters, leaders, and storm water piping to convey water from the building to the site. Ninety-five percent of the cost was accounted for by architecture's simple function as a shelter: structure, walls, windows, roofs, and interior walls and finishes. Systems constituted only 5 percent of the economic expenditure.

In 1900, architecture was no machine, and the soon to be born metaphor for architecture as a machine to live in was as yet only a dream. For such simple structures, many of the advantages afforded by off-site fabrication did not pertain, and thus the economic underpinning for success was not present. Neither time nor money were saved in sufficient quantity, and quality and scope were not enhanced. In a relatively simple dormitory 100 years later, by comparison, there are now at least 10 additional systems: radiant heating, ventilation, and automated controls; indoor plumbing for bathrooms, kitchens, drinking fountains, and custodial closets; regular electrical power and emergency power; lighting; telephone and data connections; security and fire detection, alarms, and suppression. The amount of money spent on these systems as a percentage of total cost has increased more than fivefold in the past 100 years— from 5 percent to 27 percent. For complex new structures such as

1899-1901, Little Hall, Princeton University

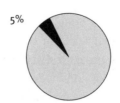

5%

Building Systems as
Percentage of Total Cost

BUILDING SYSTEMS:
Fireplace Heating
Storm Drain System

1992, Science & Technology Center, Rider College

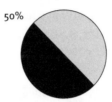

50%

Building Systems as
Percentage of Total Cost

BUILDING SYSTEMS:
HVAC
  - Radiators
  - A.C. or F.C.U.
  - Ventilation
  - Controls
  - Exhaust
Plumbing
Power
Lighting
Emergency Lighting
Telephone
Data
Security
Fire Alarm
Fire Suppression
Water Purification
Gas Distribution

INCREASING COMPLEXITY

BUILDINGS ARE BECOMING MACHINES   *The cost of mechanical systems is now approaching 50 percent of a building's overall cost. The complex weaving of all these systems would be more precisely and economically executed in a factory environment than on a building site.*

laboratories, the proportion of total expenditure attributable to systems can be as high as 50 percent—fully one-half of the economic cost.

We have only now—100 years after the first articulation of the dream—developed an architecture that is truly a machine to live and work in. Yet where is the vision now that we have the machine? We still build as though our buildings were all bricks and mortar and no systems. In truth, so many miles of pipe, wire, and duct now course through our buildings that the systems have become the unwitting, unseen structure of our architecture.

There are now so many systems that they could hold the entire building up.

The complex weaving of infrastructure, system by system, mile by mile, is not a pretty sight in conventional field-built construction. It is largely negotiated in real time, in the field, among several different subcontractors all competing for the same limited space. In the end, the building is nothing more than a prototype, a flawed yet permanent trial.

Building large portions of our architectural machines off site now makes sense, and the current machinery of architecture demands a new approach. Integrated component assembly off site makes sense for complex systems in ways that it does not for mere shelter alone. The entire scheduling enterprise can be changed through the medium of off-site fabrication. We can now substitute a new temporal order of simultaneous scheduling for the old tyranny of sequential fabrication by one system at a time. We can improve the efficiency and productivity of the environment in which large portions of our buildings are made and thereby lower cost. We can fully integrate systems and improve the quality, features, and scope of our architecture as an armature and envelope for the machinery it houses.

VI

MASS CUSTOMIZATION
OF ARCHITECTURE

NATURE'S MASS CUSTOMIZATION

COMPLEX AND FULL OF CONTRADICTIONS   *Wilson "Snowflake" Bentley said in 1925 that "Every crystal was a masterpiece of design and no one design was ever repeated." (Image: National Oceanic and Atmospheric Administration/Department of Commerce.)*

FROM DELL WITH LOVE

You have a choice. Build architecture the way Henry Ford showed you to build automobiles at the turn of the twentieth century—but, by the way, you can only use one type of structure, one type of window, one type of interior finish, one type of exterior cladding. Or, build architecture the way Michael Dell builds his computers at the beginning of the twenty first century. Use what is appropriate. Let the customers have it their way. And have it faster, better, and cheaper.

At this time, in this world, Ford's "one size fits all," no longer makes for a successful product, project, or service. The *raison d'etre* behind Ford's way of building cars was essentially to provide a product to a large pool of potential customers, a rare opportunity in this day and age. Low cost was essential to convince Ford's public to buy his product. Since the cars were designed and constructed simply, modest quality for low cost was generally easy to achieve by the repetitive assembly method. Things that did not work were easily fixed. Ford's idea of choice, "you can have any color you want as long as it is black" kept marketing and transaction costs low. Millions of copies of the exact same car were made for over two decades.

In this century we desire choice, expression, individuality, and the ability to change our minds at the last minute. The new client mandate for choice has already swept through the commercial products industry. Dell Computer company, Nike shoe company, Swatch watch manufacturers, and the automobile and apparel industries have organized their companies to meet that mandate by providing choices, in real time, at lower cost, and higher quality. These product attributes aim at securing an increased market share for their brand. By breaking down their products into small parts these companies can assemble the parts to meet the demand for choice. Through supply-chain management, achieved by electronic software, each of these companies can tailor to your needs the exact product of your choice and ship it in a reasonable time at a reasonable cost. Millions of products are sold daily with slight to full differ-

FROM DELL WITH LOVE

MADE TO ORDER   *The Dell Corporation was started in 1984 with Michael Dell's revolutionary idea to sell custom built computers directly to the customer. Mass customization was born.*

entiation. With this manufacturing model, capitalist market theories respond to the widest public desire.

At KieranTimberlake, we asked ourselves why this idea is not pursued in architecture and construction. Why do we continue to see costs escalate in making buildings at a rate exceeding the national average cost of living? Why are we consistently forced to make design decisions on the basis of costs that result in less choice, less customization, more standardization, and less quality? Why are we faced with numerous quality issues at the end of the construction process, solved only by reams of paper and countless hours of time? Compounding our frustration is the drive of our industry professional organizations to limit our involvement with the means and methods of construction. As architects we find it difficult to stop designing and not involve ourselves in the construction process. We are not satisfied with the status quo. Design continues through construction.

We have found that mass customization offers real change for architecture and construction, if no panacea. Unlike Henry Ford, we do not imagine that "one size fits all" will work for all designs, all projects, at all sites, with all clients. The projects that follow demonstrate our attempts to meet the new client mandate in a variety of building components and one entire building, in which we investigate the viability and vitality of fabricating architecture a new way. From doors to walls, vanities to full bathrooms, and to a full building, we have attempted to answer our own questions. The real change we call for cannot occur, however, without a beginning. It is time to begin.

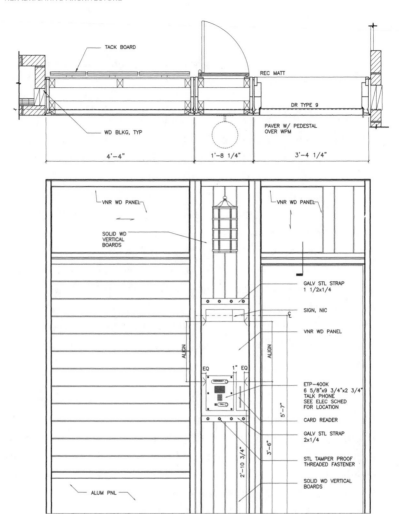

DUKE DOORS - CONSTRUCTION DOCUMENTS

SECTION AND ELEVATION *The strategy here responds to the programmatic evolution of a planar architectural transitional element to a site of technical infrastructure and interaction that requires volume. The solution stays within Duke's collegiate gothic vocabulary while developing the door as a cabinet system with larger and deeper jambs that contain enough volume to accept current and future devices. A lockable door allows access for device maintenance and replacement. The intention was to install all of this equipment in modules that had been prewired in the shop and could be delivered to the site as one unit. The contractor supported this design strategy but not to the point that fully realized its potential.*

DUKE DOORS - SITE INSTALLED

PRODUCTION   *Due to existing procurement systems and contracts already established at Duke, the devices and wiring were to be supplied by a number of different contractors who were unable to coordinate with the door carpenter's off-site shop. While all of the millwork was constructed off site as a single unit to be installed in the field, all of the wiring and device installation happened in the field. This being an early venture into off-site production, these shortcomings may have been the result of our design approach. The design was well into the construction document stage when the idea of off-site production arose and as a result the design was detailed in the manner of conventional construction that then had to be interpreted by the fabricator.*

ASSA ABLOY DOORS - PARTS

PARTS *This project was a spin-off from experiments at Duke. Originally, there were two goals for this project: The first was to integrate the wiring and equipment for security, handicap accessibility, and fire detection into a door and frame system. The second goal was to install the entire system in one piece at the end of the job. This second aim arose from a desire to avoid the typical problem of door hanging. Doors are among the last parts to be installed in buildings.*

ASSA ABLOY DOORS - MODULES

ASSEMBLIES *Unfortunately, this is usually the time of maximum congestion at the job site. All of the building trades are trying to use the same doorway to rush in and finish their work, and they are all trying to do it as the door is being hung. If one could eliminate all of the wiring and device installation from the field time, this job could become safer and achieve a higher quality. At a later point, a third goal of meeting fire ratings was added, but it became a difficult design problem because rating systems are advanced through testing and not through a preexisting set of rules that outline construction and detailing. Wiring penetrations and frame attachments that do not mesh well with existing fire-rating strategies remain a design problem still to be solved.*

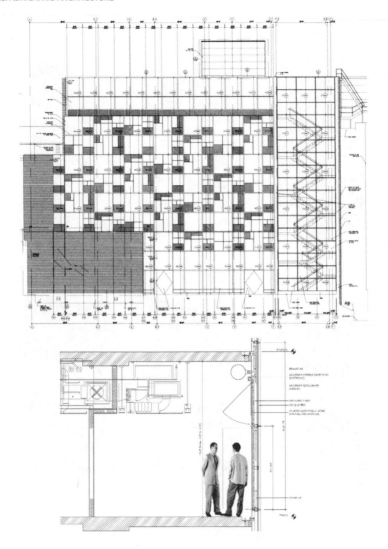

LEVINE WALL - THE CONCEPT

ELEVATION AND SECTION   *The design problem was to provide the most transparent wall possible on a site in the middle of a dense block of introspective masonry buildings. Energy code requirements were met by an active, unitized, pressure-equalized, double-skin curtain wall. The façade comprises an external double-glazed glass unit, a circulating air cavity with integral electronics and blind, and an internal single-glazed unit. The cavity acts a plenum through which room return air is circulated and extracted by the HVAC system. The intermediate blind reflects incident radiation and, along with the inner glass unit, keeps the room at a comfortable temperature.*

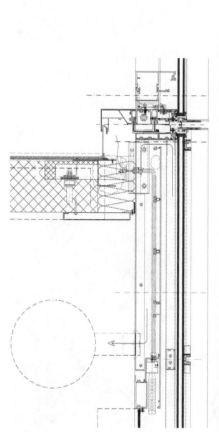

LEVINE WALL - PROTOTYPE DETAILS

CONVINCING THE CLIENT *Because the system was technically complex, Permasteelisa was the only company capable of producing the wall. The client was interested, but skeptical. They were against proprietary systems, and there were also concerns about a foreign product being unproven in the United States. Additional research was undertaken to determine the system's value. For example, what would the trade-off be if a standard curtain wall were used? Would heating and cooling loads increase? Would spandrel glass be needed? After presenting our analysis and fending off the value engineering proposals, the client came to the decision that the active curtain wall resulted in lower energy cost and better long-term value.*

LEVINE WALL - INSTALLATION

AT THE SITE *Since the first row of panels was critical to establish alignment for each elevation, Permasteelisa trained union steelworkers in the technology of installation. Coordination of materials and joints was also critical. The installation sequence should have started with the dimensionally precise curtain wall, but due to Permasteelisa's production schedule, construction of the brick had to commence before the windows had even been delivered to the site. Detailing difficulties arose where the brick, with its greater variety in dimensions, did not provide an even line to join the curtain wall, which is engineered with much higher precision.*

LEVINE WALL - COMPLETION IN 7 WEEKS

MOVE IN DAY *Besides being an energy-efficient choice, this was a mass-customizable one as well. A wide range of mullion patterns could be designed without disrupting Permasteelisa's production process. The units came to the site pretested and preassembled, which saved the limited lay-down space. An additional benefit of the mass-customized system was that it did not require a sealant. Gaskets and precision metalwork installed in the shop provided better quality control at joints, which resulted in not just a sealed insulation system, but also a sealed acoustical system. The quality control was exceptional. The university realized a beautiful 40-year wall, and people inside have greater comfort with control over their surroundings.*

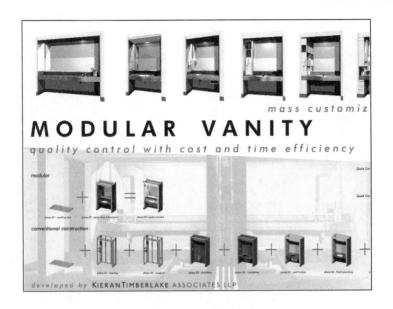

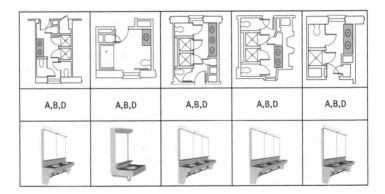

MODULAR VANITY - STUDY FOR DUPONT

VARIATIONS *An interest in rethinking architectural problems combined with DuPont's interest in selling more Corian led to this project. DuPont was interested in expanding its market from single materials to packaged complete systems. Bathrooms were a logical choice, as they are a critical-path item. Every trade on the job is trying to squeeze into one tiny room all at the same time: plumbers, electricians, drywallers, tilers, and carpenters all need access to the space many times at different stages in the job. While DuPont's involvement with the lodging industry had been productive, they were encountering resistance on the construction site. The usual problems of inherited field conditions were demanding an enormous amount of their time and effort to solve.*

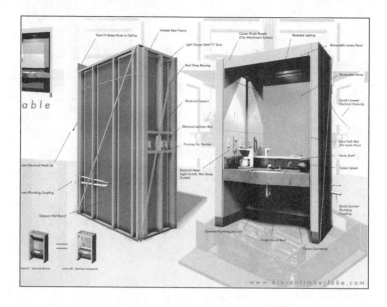

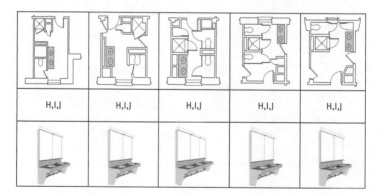

H,I,J	H,I,J	H,I,J	H,I,J	H,I,J

MODULAR VANITY - MASS CUSTOMIZATION

VARIATIONS *The similarities between this product for the hotel industry and renovation work at Yale's residential colleges were quickly apparent, and DuPont was convinced to fund a prototype. Yale's need for eight different vanities in 53 bathrooms was a perfect candidate for this exercise in mass customization. The design process for the vanity prototype was different from the usual interaction between architect and contractor because there were no sketches, CDs, or shop drawings of any kind. The relation between architect and contractor, however, was more what you might expect. For instance, for them, it was good to hide seams. Seamless construction is what Corian wants to be, whereas we would have liked to expose the joints between parts.*

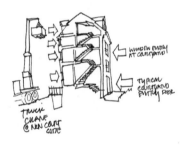

PIERSON VANITY - INSTALLATION AND DETAILS

Where the architect wanted an aluminum structure to save weight, the fabricator pushed for steel because it is easy to work with.

Yale came to see the prototype and was convinced of its relevence to the renovation of their residential college. They were pleased with the quality of the fabrication and its plumbing and pleased as well to learn that the prototype offered a savings of $100,000 over the field construction of the 53 bathrooms. There was really nothing to sell and the owner embraced the concept.

PIERSON VANITY - PROTOTYPE

Installation with a crane turned out to be impractical, but a computer simulation proved to Yale that the vanities could be carried up the stairs if the design were modified to make the mirror/light unit demountable. Naturally, since work traditionally performed in the field is being replaced with a factory assembly, union concerns have arisen. To resolve the problem, the nonunion shop fabricator agreed to hire union laborers to assist in the vanity's construction so the construction manager could meet the terms of his labor agreement. The design was approached from the front, with the usual aesthetic concerns; approaching the design problem from the infrastructure side could lead to further advances in the quality and economy of the parts kit.

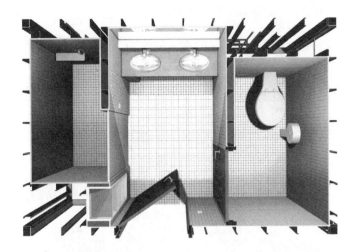

CORNELL BATHROOM - CONCEPT

PLAN AND HALL VIEWS *A series of new residence halls for Cornell University presented the opportunity to build the entire bathroom module at a factory. Each unit would be craned into position and hooked up before the building was closed in.*

Issues beyond simple construction arise when designing an entire room as a seperate unit. Fire codes dictated a number of shaft conditions that took a lot of negotiation to resolve. Plus, combining field with factory construction resulted in a number of double-wall conditions, adding to the cost.

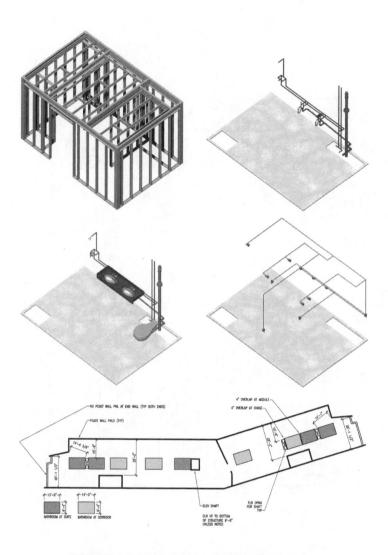

CORNELL BATHROOM - INFRASTRUCTURE

COMPONENT DIAGRAMS AND KEY PLAN *This design entered the game late as an addendum and probably did not get the attention needed to make it succeed. Both the university and the construction manager were skeptical. There was very little time to convince them of the potential for higher quality and lower cost for the 350 bathrooms that would eventually be built. As a result, the estimates from the contractor came in high, and the client decided on traditional construction methods. The client and contractor's introduction to off-site construction must start early in the design process.*

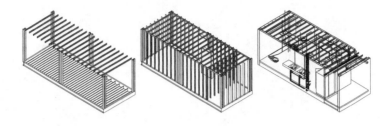

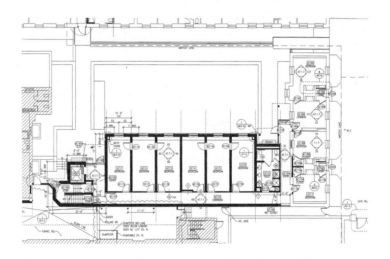

PIERSON MODULAR BUILDING - DOCUMENTS

MODULE AND PLAN *The scheme for this small addition to a residential college was near resolution before the idea of off-site fabrication ever occurred. Located on a restricted site, with a construction schedule constrained by adjacent renovations and the university's classes, this project was a natural candidate for an off-site construction approach. The site is the main staging area for basement demolition and roof-work on an adjacent existing building. In addition, utilities need to be installed in the courtyard before the addition is constructed, so there was a real effort to coordinate the use of the small site for other parts of the project as well. As a result, the entire structure must be craned into place during the university's spring break.*

PIERSON MODULAR BUILDING - FABRICATION

SHOP JOINTS   *Ultimately, the savings only worked out to about 17 percent less than traditional construction methods, but both Yale and the construction manager believed it was the right way to go, given the site restrictions and the potential time savings. Another issue was the construction manager's contract. Traditionally, the construction manager is paid based on how much is constructed on site. Understandably, the client did not want to double-pay for Pierson and said a different cost model was required. A compromise was reached easily due to the addition's small size, but in the future a new paradigm for construction contracts will be required for larger construction projects.*

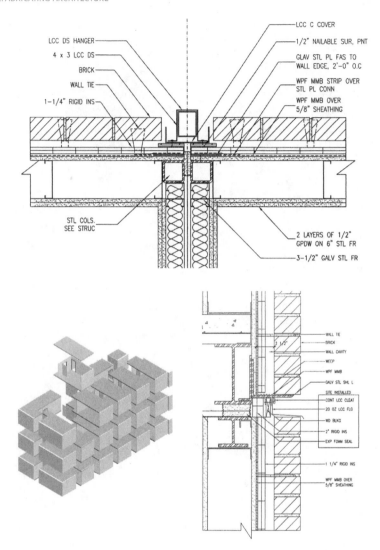

LCC DS HANGER
4 x 3 LCC DS
BRICK
WALL TIE
1-1/4" RIGID INS

LCC C COVER
1/2" NAILABLE SUR, PNT
GLAV STL PL FAS TO
WALL EDGE, 2'-0" O.C
WPF MMB STRIP OVER
STL PL CONN
WPF MMB OVER
5/8" SHEATHING

STL COLS.
SEE STRUC

2 LAYERS OF 1/2"
GPDW ON 6" STL FR
3-1/2" GALV STL FR

WALL TIE
BRICK
WALL CAVITY
WEEP
WPF MMB
GALV STL SHL L
SITE INSTALLED,
CONT LCC CLEAT
20 OZ LCC FLG
WD BLKG
2" RIGID INS
EXP FOAM SEAL

1 1/4" RIGID INS

WPF MMB OVER
5/8" SHEATHING

PIERSON MODULAR BUILDING - JOINING

SITE JOINTS   *Politically, this project has been a difficult foray into mass customization. A lot of people had to be convinced of the efficacy of the approach: the New Haven Building Trades Council, 20 people at Yale, the construction manager, Kullman (the modular assembly company), the fire marshal, and the New Haven building inspector. Everyone had to be convinced that modular assembly was the right way to go.*

PIERSON MODULAR BUILDING - INTERIORS

The frame is designed to accommodate seismic loads, not because New Haven is a potential epicenter, but because these units have to sustain a 500-mile trip on a flatbed and the stresses of being lifted 70 feet into the air. The units are punch-listed at the factory, and after the building inspector has signed off, they are sealed in shrink wrap for delivery to the site. The exterior brick detail between each unit is not designed for expansion purposes, as each frame is bolted to each adjacent frame and they will act as a unit. In addition, there were concerns that mortar mixed in the New Jersey factory would not match mortar mixed on the New Haven site. Kullman assured everyone that they were quite accustomed to matching shop with field conditions.

VII

EVOLUTION, NOT REVOLUTION

BOEING WORLDWIDE CONSTRUCTS

A NEW USE FOR AN OLD PLANT   *After several years of trying to find a new use for the Everett, WA, 747/777 manufacturing plant, Boeing Constructs decided to plunge into the modular building industry. Already fully equipped to handle construction of very large chunks of aircraft, it took little time to get started building. (Image: Boeing.)*

SURVEYING THE SITE

SIMULTANEOUS CONSTRUCTION   *While Boeing Constructs begins fabricating their home in the factory, the client is having their new plot of land surveyed for the impending preparation site work.*

7.1   FABRICATION, NOT CONSTRUCTION

Let us imagine ourselves forward in time a decade from now. It is Autumn 2013. On a beautiful afternoon, we enjoy driving in your new hydrogen-powered Cad-Wire, the latest Cadillac version of the GM Hy-Wire car first shown at the 2002 Detroit International Automobile Show. We approach the main gate of a massive complex of buildings in Everett, Washington. No one is in sight. The worldwide buzz is that something big is going on here: Boeing has found a use for this recently unused plant, but it is not for airplanes.

"The Puget Sound area and the state of Washington are now facing one of their worst nightmares—the possibility that Boeing, its biggest employer will move final assembly of its next wide-body jet to another state." (*The New York Times*, June 10, 2003)

Since you have always been interested in technology and process, you know that for nearly eight years Boeing has tried to find new uses for both its old 737 assembly plant in Renton, Washington, and this 747/777 assembly plant here in Everett. In 2001, the Boeing Company had relocated its world headquarters to Chicago in a move that re-energized and reinvigorated the company. Now nimble and quick to seize the advantage in both its own market and in others, Boeing's worldwide value is currently double that of GE's. The move to the center of the country strategically disconnected the company from its two former mainstays of commercial airplane assembly in the United States. For the past decade, Boeing's long-term strategy has been to move assembly worldwide and to make airplanes wherever the planes were to be delivered. Now, with over 400 units of all sizes of aircraft to be delivered to China Airways, Boeing has put in place the final step in its assembly policy. Build, assemble, and deliver locally. Locally today means right on the doorstep of each airline that purchases the aircraft. Boeing's DCAC, Catia CAD/CAM, and other process software, together with its network of suppliers of modules and parts now enable Boeing and its partners to ship instantaneously anywhere in the world, including for example, Toulouse and Paris, right on Airbus's doorstep.

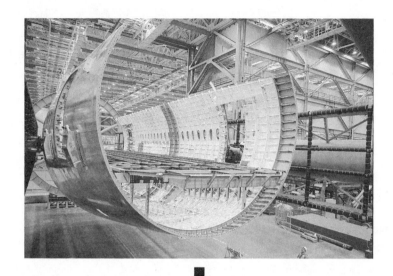

A SECTION IS A SECTION

TRANSFERRING EXPERTISE *It was quite easy for Boeing Constructs to transition from assembling airplanes to fabricating buildings. As was true for aircraft, they found that it was best to build using large modular chunks and take advantage of component assemblies to simplify tasks and expedite completion. In addition, they implemented their system of eboms and mboms for all parts. By simply scanning a barcode, a panel on the factory floor displays an ebom that provides the detailed design facts: length, width, thickness, materials, weight, strength in bending, shear strength, etc. In addition, a solid model is associated with each part that shows its relation to the whole assembly and from which an mbom can be derived at the click of a button. (Image: Boeing.)*

After closing its last two largest assembly plants near Seattle in 2005, Boeing had decentralized its aircraft assembly process globally. Boeing realized that abandoning its plants, particularly in the northwest where it had been the largest employer for a century, meant leaving behind a loyal and committed workforce. The Renton plant was situated near rail lines, an airfield, and a port, and the Everett plant was situated near rail and a 15,000-foot runway. Both these sites offered excellent shipping opportunities for whatever the plants produced. But what would its product be?

In a hunt for a new product for their plants, market research undertaken by the newly resurgent company uncovered a worldwide construction market that was clearly foundering for lack of integration and innovation. Boeing knew how to assemble very large, complex, habitable structures—pressurized enclosures that were able to fly faster than 600 miles per hour, accommodate 550 people, and last for more than 30 years. These structures were products that had changed industry design, assembly, and delivery processes worldwide. Renton and Everett and its experience in assembling complex structures had given Boeing an idea. Instead of aircraft, Boeing would now use Renton and Everett to build mass-customized buildings from components, modules, and grand blocks that had all their systems fully integrated. They would then ship these completed chunks of buildings worldwide. Boeing Worldwide Constructs, a new global assembler of whole buildings, instantly began competing with Skanska, Takenaka, and Bovis Lend Lease.

As we approach the gate in Everett for our two o'clock tour, a strangely silent plant faces us across from the main gate. Can this really be a construction site? The only sounds that reach us come from the large freight aircraft landing or taking off every five minutes from the airstrip behind the plant. Virtually every one of the old parking lots has been removed. The old workers' commute to the plant by car has been replaced by a rail shuttle that loops through

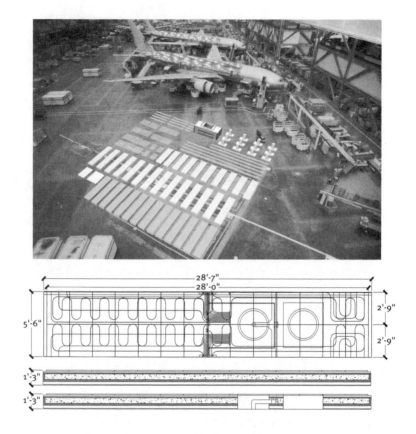

FROM 1,267 PIECES TO 80 COMPONENTS

THE NEW MATHEMATICS OF COMPONENT ASSEMBLY *Boeing Constructs's methods resulted in a kit of parts totaling 80 pieces for this particular building. These 80 components can be easily erected in a matter of days. To traditionally "stick build" the same house would require at least 1,267 major pieces and take a few months to assemble. The drawing below the photo shows a plan and elevation of a flooring component on the factory floor in the photo.*

Everett, Seattle, and Renton at 30-minute intervals to carry workers, suppliers, and customers. The one remaining parking lot is small and reserved for tours. Our tour, about to begin, assembles in the front lobby, where a gallery of photographs documents the company's accomplishments in design and assembly over the past five decades. Images of the 707, 747, 777, the space shuttle, and the international space station are here, along with the 40-story-high 1 Parkway Place in Philadelphia, the final five buildings in Battery Park City, New York—averaging 60 stories each—and diverse other building complexes in Shanghai, Kowloon, Delhi, Tangiers, and other cities around the globe.

As we board the tour surreys and they lurch to a start, we may think back to tours of half a century ago at the Ford Motor Company's River Rouge automobile plant. Back then, surrey Jeeps pulled a trailer train that crawled through stygian conditions. The noise: the mind-numbing noise of the stamping plants and the assembly lines; the dirt: the inescapable, choking soot of the foundry; the disorder: the jumble of ill-fitting and wasted parts tossed onto the assembly floor and the shiny cars filthy with grease and grime from the assembly process; the smells: the caustic stench of glues, rubbers, fuels, chrome-dipping vats, and paint lines; the crepuscular light: the grim, medieval quality of the light barely penetrating inaccessible, filthy windows high above and only intermittently augmented by dim, bare lightbulbs projecting uneven light onto the assembly lines. All of these chaotic and disagreeable memories flood our mind in anticipation of today's tour.

The surreys pass through a giant, 11-story, moving door that yawns hugely to accept us. First impressions are everything. Light, order, healthful and comfortable air, and the subdued hum of purposeful activity greet us. The interior environment of the assembly building

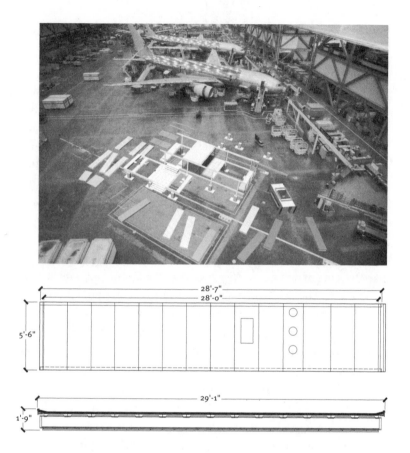

ASSEMBLING THE CHASSIS AND COMPONENTS

TEST BUILDING *Perhaps the greatest advantage of Boeing Constructs's methods is that they fully assemble each piece of the design on the factory floor before shipping the component out for erection on site. This ensures that each will perform properly and that there will be no issues with joining in the field, where time is far more costly. The plan and section above show one of the integrated ceiling modules of the project on the factory floor.*

is clean, as it would have been for the assembly of 777s a decade ago. In the four corners of this cavernous plant, various multiple-story sections of buildings are being assembled and then disassembled to ready them for shipping worldwide. All the major subcomponent module suppliers are here: Permasteelisa, Chandit, Assa Abloy, Praxtix, USGypsum, Trane, USMetals, Dow, DuPont, and Kalix. These companies, which represent a cross-section of trades, suppliers of materials, and assemblers, are all at work either here in the plant or immediately adjacent to it. Through acquisition, all of these brands have become global conglomerates that supply materials and assemble components. Many have incorporated large construction-management companies into their corporate structure. Over the past seven years, an evolution has occurred in construction assembly. No longer is the world governed by the 16 McGraw-Hill Sweets Catalog divisions. Instead, through supplier shakeouts and realignments, the 16 divisions have now become seven assembly sets or modules. These seven sets, representing the Tier 1 suppliers, are supported by more than 30 Tier 1.5 and 50 Tier 2 subsuppliers. The lower-tier suppliers, like their counterparts in the aerospace, automobile, and shipbuilding industries, contribute the design and preassembly of major components and modules.

Beyond the agreeable atmosphere in the plant, one of the first things we notice is that the workers are productive, comfortable, and safe. Over half of the workers assembling large portions of buildings indoors are women—one of the first signs of the recent modernization of the construction culture. OSHA standards are not only met but exceeded, establishing new guidelines for worker safety. The plant has been open for more than two years, yet it has never had an accident. It affords year-round production without weather delays or environmental and occupational hazards. Hard hats are nonexistent. The workers all wear jumper uniforms colored to represent their company's team colors—safety orange for Boeing

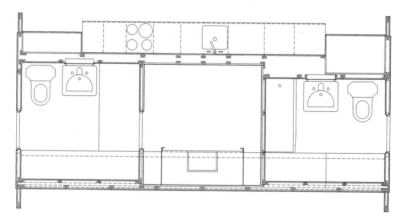

ADDING CHUNKS

SUPPLYING COMPONENTS JUST IN TIME   *The use of extensive component assemblies fabricated in adjacent parts of the production facility or in the facilities of subcontracted parts suppliers is one of the crowning achievements of Boeing Construct's new building paradigm. Kitchen and bathroom units are being fully outfitted, while floor and ceiling modules are fabricated and test-joined to the frame. The result is an architectural first, scope and quality are finally exceeding time and costs of construction. The images above show the largest component of the current project, the kitchen core module.*

Worldwide, blue for Permasteelisa, grey for Praxtix, and so on. In this building, the work of assembly is carried out 23 hours a day, 6 days a week in three shifts that compress the time required for assembly to delivery of the completed buildings. The economic benefit of this condensed schedule is huge. Despite 4 percent cost-of-living increases each year for the past decade—totaling a consumer price index increase of nearly 50 percent—real building costs have increased by only 10 percent over the same period. Our guide tells us that the process from conception through design, completion, and delivery takes roughly half the time that the total on-site building process took only a decade ago. The use of integrated component assemblies has streamlined the number of parts going into a building and in the process has created a profitable, sustainable construction industry. As if that weren't enough, we are told, scope and quality are finally exceeding time and costs for the first time in the history of construction.

For an hour the tour wends it way throughout the plant. On one section of the plant floor, chassis of buildings are readied on low, electric, multitiered transport beds that are relocated precisely by robots from one section of the plant to another by a GPS. The chassis includes the main structure of the building and its mechanical, electrical, plumbing, and data rough-ins. Whole portions of the chassis come together preassembled by Praxis, Chandit, and Trane. Before assembly, the infrastructure is tested. Building inspectors work side by side with assembly workers to ensure high quality and full compliance with codes and standards.

Once we see the components of the chassis that are complete, we begin to have a vision of the architecture to come. Whether the architect is Gehry Global, SOM, or a moderately sized Philadelphia firm working worldwide, the construction assembly easily absorbs the complexities of their designs. The chassis framework allows for the total integration of systems while eliminating redundant, costly,

PACKAGING AND SHIPPING

NEXT DAY AIR   *With the runway and loading areas just outside the factory doors, shipping of building modules is very efficient. The various components are categorized, codified, and packaged for travel and simply rolled out to the proper cargo flight. (Image: AFP/Corbis.)*

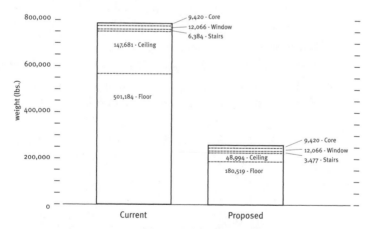

MATERIALS SUBSTITUTIONS

LIGHTENING THE LOAD   *Building modules potentially need to be transported great distances; therefore, weight is a major design constraint for Boeing Constructs. With this particular project, the weight needed to be decreased to a third of its traditional weight through material substitution. The lighter a project can be made the cheaper it will be to transport.*

and hard-to-maintain building components. No matter what the design, Boeing Worldwide Constructs, through its computer visualization, can work with each architecture firm to anticipate assembly issues, maintenance problems, and the design opportunities that can benefit the building long term. After the chassis is complete, interior and exterior prosthetics are added in the form of modules and components, the precursors to finishing each grand block. Assa Abloy, USGypsum, and DuPont are among the major suppliers in these areas. As we move down a service corridor nearly a half-mile long, we see 50 completed chassis being outfitted with prosthetics. We are told that once complete, these 50 components, along with 21 others already completed, will form a new 70-story building in Toronto. Since the site, foundation, and infrastructure work proceeds in parallel with the assembly, this new, tall office building will take only six months to construct.

Upon the installation of the prosthetics and the assembly of the major subcomponents, the exterior and interior finish systems are applied. Permasteelisa, USMetals, and Kalix each outfit exterior and interior systems within the blocks. Some of the parts for these components are supplied globally, flown in from Italy, New York State, and South America and delivered just in time for use. Glass systems come from Asia. The deliveries are packaged within air containers, some with UPS and FedEx labels on them, others with proprietary identification labels from their respective companies. No parts are lost or wasted. Everything is tracked and properly placed. Workers protect the finish of individual sections as they are completed in order to avoid the mishaps to finish systems common in field-built assemblies. Parts are never damaged. The smart component assemblies that must work mechanically or electrically do so immediately, since they were tested before arriving at the plant for assembly.

DAY 1 - DELIVERIES AT THE SITE

YOU'VE GOT MAIL   *On-site assembly begins as the modules arrive by truck. In the previous weeks while the modules were being fabricated, the site was prepared, foundations were laid, utilities put in place, and landscaping completed. Now it is simply a matter of opening the packages and assembling the bar-coded puzzle.*

DAY 2 - REASSEMBLING THE COMPONENTS

A HOUSE EMERGES FROM 9 TO 5   *With a crew of just three contractors, the on-site assembly technicians crane all of the modules into place and seal the connections. By the end of one working day the entire house is erected and ready for quick-coupling to the utilities.*

As each completed grand block of building emerges on its transport carrier, it is taken to the shipping staging area that we first came to upon entering the building at the beginning of our tour. Here, up to seven stories of structures are lifted off their transport by an overhead crane, a relic of the old days of Boeing when this crane was used to lift 75-foot by 45-foot sections of 777 aircraft fuselage, each weighing 150,000 pounds. The overhead crane lifts each section into its proper position relative to its adjacent grand blocks. These sections are preassembled and then disassembled, placed back on their transport, and packaged for shipping. Each is heat shrink-wrapped, affording a last layer of protection. The grand blocks are then rolled out through one of the main doors onto the tarmac at Everett, placed on palettes for loading into a Boeing 747 SuperStretch or Airbus A340x, usually along with two to three other blocks, and airlifted to an airport near the building site. At Everett, as at Renton, rail lines are heavily used to move building blocks cross-country and regionally. Occasionally, the building components are shipped through the Port of Seattle, if they are too large for a plane. We watch as three building blocks are loaded in only two hours into the large planes that swallow whole building pieces as easily as a child gobbling up a TastyKake snack cake.

Boeing Worldwide Constructs now dominates an industry that had as recently as only a decade ago faced declining quality and increasing costs. Except for an occasional highly idiosyncratic building program, this new way of building has now replaced the old conventional construction in the modern world. Now, when the world thinks of building, it thinks of low-maintenance, long-life structures assembled from component packages that are delivered on schedule and on budget. The world thinks of the reification of the dream they sought to produce architecture at the highest quality ever achieved.

DAY 3 - TURNING OVER THE KEYS

ANOTHER SATISFIED CUSTOMER   *After the final connections have been made and the sealants cured, the client receives the keys. On this serene plot of land the formerly disconnected pieces of the puzzle snap into focus. Floor, wall, and core. The Boeing Constructs house is a twenty-first century interpretation of Mies van der Rohe's Farnsworth House. This interpretation looks the same but was erected in three days and has more performance features and costs less relative to the original.*

7.2   OUR FABRICATION

In 2001, KieranTimberlake Associates undertook an internal research project to virtually reconstruct the Farnsworth House, designed in 1947 by Mies van der Rohe. We used new processes and new materials as part of our MB2010 (Masters Building: 2010) research initiative. The intent of this project was to reduce the number of parts constructed on site in the Farnsworth House and to incorporate materials that van der Rohe would not have had at his disposal in 1950. By integrating these new processes—preassembly of components, off-site construction and the use of new materialities—it was our goal to offer a higher quality and more lasting future for an icon of architecture. A report entitled *Component Assembly of Mies van der Rohe's Farnsworth House* was completed in March 2002. The traditional assembly of the house involved more than 1,267 parts coming together on site. The component assembly speculation reduced the overall number of parts assembled on site to somewhere between 22 and 48 components, depending upon the inclusion or elimination of infrastructure.

GRP (glass reinforced plastic) was substituted for concrete and steel components wherever possible to lighten the overall weight of the structure, add durability, and increase assembly opportunities. By making substitutions for conventional materials with new, contemporary materials, the overall weight of the structure was reduced by 60 percent. Aerogel was introduced as a composite within the glass curtain wall to increase energy efficiency. Systems and component infrastructure were integrated to minimize on-site trade coordination, improve assembly quality and minimize the number of overall joints that might come together in a final assembly. The overall structure would initially be preassembled offsite in a quality controlled environment in order to understand final assembly procedures, and anticipate any final quality control issues prior to crating, wrapping, and shipping. Through a virtual process the punch-list, the bane of every architect, constructor, and supplier, has been eliminated.

COMPONENT ASSEMBLY

THE NEW PARADIGM *Boeing Constructs method of fabrication and assembly has revolutionized architecture, or rather evolutionized architecture. Construction is simpler, faster, more precise, and less expensive. What Le Corbusier did not realize and Boeing Constructs did was that to create a machine to live in you need to build it as you would a machine.*

This fictional account of the Farnsworth House off-site construction and assembly in Everett, Washington, presumes opportunities for a worldwide assembler such as Boeing to engage in a world of construction that demands innovation and improvement. Innovations can evolve from within a process or be transferred from other processes through assimilation, mimicry, or wholesale revolution. We demand transfer. We invite the world of construction to begin anew with these processes that can make everyone's world and the architect's work better.

STEPEHN KIERAN, *FAIA, FAAR*

JAMES TIMBERLAKE, *FAIA, FAAR*

ABOUT THE AUTHORS

In 1984 Stephen Kieran, FAIA, FAAR, and James Timberlake, FAIA, FAAR, founded the firm KieranTimberlake Associates LLP, located in Philadelphia. KieranTimberlake Associates LLP has been awarded 40 design awards during the past 20 years, including two Gold Medals and two Distinguished Building Awards from the American Institute of Architects.

Stephen Kieran, received his Bachelor's degree from Yale University, magna cum laude, and his Master of Architecture from the University of Pennsylvania.

James Timberlake, received his Bachelor's degree from the University of Detroit, with honors, and his Master of Architecture from the University of Pennsylvania, with honors.

Stephen Kieran and James Timberlake were recipients of the Rome Prize (in 1981 and 1983 respectively) from the American Academy in Rome, and have served as Eero Saarinen Distinguished Professor of Design at Yale University. They were awarded the inaugural 2001 Benjamin Latrobe Fellowship for architectural design research by the AIA College of Fellows. They are also the Max Fisher Chair recipients at the University of Michigan for Spring 2004. They currently serve as Adjunct Professors at the University of Pennsylvania School of Design where they lead a graduate research studio that explores the emerging interface between architecture as high art and the integration of developing technologies in materials science and product engineering.

They lecture internationally about the processes and methods that underlie transfer technologies and what has been their involvement in this new architecture. Their firm's work has been published and featured in *Manual, The Architecture of KieranTimberlake*, (Princeton Architectural Press, 2002); and numerous publications including *Architectural Record*, Cambridge University's *Architectural Research Quarterly, Interiors, Interior Design, WIRED Magazine*, and *The New York Times*.